Rock Guitar
For Future Stars

Books by Arlen Roth
Slide Guitar: (Oak)
How to Play Blues Guitar: (Acorn)
Nashville Guitar: (Oak)
Arlen Roth's Complete Electric Guitar (Doubleday)
Arlen Roth's Complete Acoustic Guitar
(Schirmer/Macmillan)
Heavy Metal Guitar (Schirmer Books)

Albums by Arlen Roth
Arlen Roth/Guitarist (Rounder)
Hot Pickups (Rounder)
Paint Job (Breaking Records)
Lonely St. (Flying Fish)

Rock Guitar

For Future Stars

Arlen Roth

BALLANTINE BOOKS • NEW YORK

Library of Congress Catalog Card Number: 86-90863

ISBN 0-345-32346-7

Front cover photo: Arlen Roth

Back cover photo: John Peden

Photo Illustrations: Deborah Roth, Arlen Roth

Manufactured in the United States of America

First Edition: September 1986

For my parents, whose encouragement for me to play the guitar and follow my dreams made it possible for me to get this far.

ACKNOWLEDGMENTS

For their invaluable help in preparing this book with me, I wish to thank Cheryl Woodruff, Michelle Wollmers, Elissa Altman, Anne Leiner, Steve Sterns, and Joe Dalton. Without their assistance, *Rock Guitar* wouldn't have been possible.

Contents

INTRODUCTION

Rock Guitar for Future Stars. The very mention of a book title like that is enough to make you think that this book ensures stardom for those who read it. Well, of course, it's not even remotely that simple, and in fact you may never become a star at all! One thing I can guarantee, though, is that this book *will* get you on the way to becoming a finer and more dynamic guitarist. Whether something as ephemeral as stardom will follow is up to you, but much of the groundwork you must cover will be worked through over the course of this book.

The true value and beauty of the guitar is sometimes clouded by eyes that look toward stardom. It is the love of the *instrument* that should inspire and drive you on. The guitar, after all, is quite a sensuous beast, an instrument that possesses many more "vocal" qualities than some of its counterparts, and it is held so close to one's heart that a love affair between player and instrument is inescapable! The guitar possesses many unique qualities. It can be used for chords as well as single-note work. Strings can be bent, vibrated, hammered, pulled, and generally worked up into any frenzy your heart desires, and with the aid of nearly unlimited amplification possibilities, you can get your message across as loudly or softly as you wish.

Motivation to learn is something that I hope you already have, and odds are you do, or else you wouldn't have even picked up this book. I've certainly had some *very* motivated students. When I was called upon to teach Ralph Macchio to play the guitar for the film *Crossroads*, I was expecting a "star" used to having everything handed to him on a silver platter. Fortunately, I couldn't have been more off the mark, for within minutes of meeting Ralph and completing our initial lesson, I knew that though he had never held a guitar before, he was a natural. Ralph had a desire and drive for perfection that far exceeded my expectations. We did, of course, have a movie to make, and a limited amount of time in which to learn to play the guitar, but learn he did, and *Crossroads* is a better picture because of it. Though I played all of the actual guitar parts for the soundtrack of the film and Ralph is mimicking the pieces, he can *really* play! In fact, Ralph's understanding of what I was playing, and how to interpret it, was far beyond that of some players I've met who've played for ten years! If you've got one-tenth *his* drive and motivation, you should do just fine!

I would encourage you to choose, if you haven't already, your own "guitar heroes," some player or players you would like to *emulate* and *imitate* for a while. Some possible candidates might include Eddie Van Halen, Pete Townshend, Keith Richards, Stevie Ray Vaughn, and Jeff Beck. I know that in my developing years, I was constantly drawn to my favorite players for inspiration and ideas. I always seemed to seek out the players who were a bit more esoteric, or out of the "mainstream," because I was attracted by their performances; they were doing something on the instrument that was new to my ears. Sure, The Beatles inspired me; the day after I saw their American debut on *The Ed Sullivan Show*, I combed my hair down and bought an electric guitar. Still, I was in awe more of *them* than of their style of playing. To me they represented "music as a lifestyle." Equipped with a very sharp and perceptive ear, I was soon able to hear a song by The Beatles or the Stones and say, "Ah, yes, *that*; I know just how they played *that*!" I emulated guitar heroes such as B. B. King, Chuck Berry, Buddy Guy, Carl Perkins, and Mike Bloomfield. These, for the most part, were the kind of players who were also the heroes of the Stones and Beatles. Therefore, I developed a knack for going to the *source*. Led Zeppelin was not my choice, but the people *they* listened to were.

If you have a guitar hero, don't hesitate to "be him" for a while. Learning the solos and styles of your favorite players is advisable; just keep in mind that they once did the exact same thing while working on their own sound. For example, little did I know, back in the days when I was learning from a Simon and Garfunkel record, at the age of fourteen, that I would eventually be on stage with them, playing to literally millions of people! Talk about "future guitar"!

When playing the examples in this book—or any other, for that matter—you must keep in mind that the road to becoming a great player is full of discipline, hard work, and fun! After all, what we're after here is a means of *expression*, not just a series of licks. Music is a language, one that speaks deeper than words, and you should try to derive as much as possible from each stage of your development. You must learn to be satisfied with what you know at a given time while you strive to improve. This will keep you playing, and your further development will be ensured. I can barely recall a time throughout my own experience when I thought of my learning as "practice." I would play sometimes six or seven hours a day, but it was *fun*! I was doing it simply because I loved the guitar, and I was completely turned on by the idea of making music! I hope this kind of feeling holds true for you, too.

Finally, it is important that you feel that you've accomplished something every time you've played. Try not to end on a discouraged note, though in some instances this can serve as inspiration to try even harder! In either case, be sure to set goals for yourself, and to take things slowly, one at a time. Enjoy your playing, be creative, and don't be satisfied until it sounds the way *you* want it to! Remember, practice must be *fun*, too!

Chapter One

EQUIPMENT

The Guitar: A Brief History

This six-stringed beauty has probably evoked more romance and adventure than any other instrument in history, although it isn't even that old. The guitar as we know it (or Spanish guitar, as it's been called) evolved from the earlier lute instruments sometime during the seventeenth century. When it became popular as six strings tuned E-A-D-G-B-E remains a matter of conjecture, but this is generally referred to as "Spanish" tuning, its origins quite well defined.

The guitar's involvement in American music began even before the birth of the nation. Played by Spanish sailors and Mexicans, the guitar and its various cousins were to be seen more and more throughout America's landscape, particularly in the early 1800s. Cowboys of the southwest began to pick it up from the Mexicans they would encounter, and the Spaniards who settled throughout the south were also making the guitar's presence strongly felt. C. F. Martin, perhaps America's most important and historic guitar maker, set up shop in New York around 1833, bringing over a fine tradition in handcrafted instruments from Germany. Instruments such as these were finding their way into the hands of many novices, most of whom were interested in the guitar as an accompaniment to the voice.

It wasn't until the early part of the twentieth century that the guitar developed a more important role in popular music and sophisticated single-note work was introduced to the instrument's repertoire. Players such as Nick Lucas, Eddie Lang, and Roy Smeck were among the first "solo" artists associated with the guitar to be lauded for their technical virtuosity. Other string instruments, such as the mandolin, ukelele, and banjo, enjoyed crazes, but only the guitar has had a steady ascension in popularity.

Though there were several featured guitar soloists in the early part of the twentieth century, these players were all confined to playing *acoustic*, non-amplified instruments. I say confined because in a band situation, an acoustic guitar can only be heard as a strummed, rhythm instrument, and therefore these early players were limited to solo or small-group performances. Along came the amplified guitar, however, and a man named Charlie Christian. Christian was the first true electric-guitar soloist, and his playing with the Benny Goodman Sextet was so revolutionary that his influence can still be plainly heard today.

Soon after, in the late forties, men such as Les Paul and Leo Fender were beginning to experiment with making a *solidbody* electric guitar that would eliminate feedback problems and create greater sustain for the guitarist. These guitars were made of a solid piece of wood, and contained no sound chambers. Les Paul was fast becoming a recording star through his hit records with his wife, Mary Ford, and was also the first musician to experiment with multitrack recording and overdubbing, or layering of many instrumental and vocal tracks onto one song. The guitar that he created, of course, was put out by Gibson, and since its inception in 1952, the Les Paul guitar has remained a true rock guitar classic.

Though individuals such as Paul Bigsby and Les Paul were experimenting with solidbodies, in 1948 Leo Fender, the man behind Fender guitars, issued the first "production" (mass-produced) solidbody ever, the Broadcaster (the name was later changed to Telecaster). It has remained one of the most popular instruments of all time.

Now, for the first time, a guitarist could "turn up" the volume, reach higher notes on the fretboard, and in general have more creativity available to face the changing musical scene and its challenges. It's incredible to think that the first three production solidbody guitars, the Les Paul, the Stratocaster, and the Telecaster, in spite of the countless new designs and experiments, still remain the three most popular guitar styles of all time! And they were designed before the advent of rock 'n' roll!

This all points up the fact that it's not so much the instruments that have changed, but the players themselves. There seems to be no limit to what can be done on the instrument, so let those six strings stay the same— and let your imagination fly!

The Guitar: An Anatomy Lesson

Before we begin our playing and our discussion of which guitar is best for you, let us get you acquainted with the instrument itself. The diagram on page 4 shows the parts of the guitar. Refer to it from time to time should a certain term or place on the instrument sound unfamiliar to you.

The parts of the guitar have remained fairly standard over the years. It still needs a headstock, where the strings are attached, some with six on one side, others with three on each side. There is the nut, over which the strings pass before they get to the headstock. The metal strips on top of the fingerboard that create the notes are called frets. Be sure to play *between* them, as close as possible to the higher of two frets. This will result in the cleanest, clearest tone with the least amount of effort. Electric guitars have *pickups*, which translate the sound of the metal string's vibrations into electrical impulses, while acoustic instruments rely upon their open sound chambers to project the sound of the strings. In recent times, special pickups have been developed for acoustic instruments as well, even for nylon strings. In this sense, one can see that the electric guitar's sound is derived from restraint and control of sound, while the acoustic guitar requires more physical

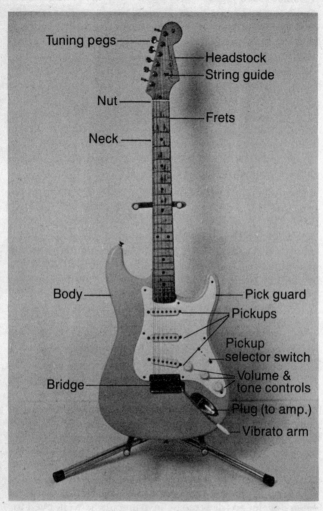

Tuning pegs

Headstock

String guide

Nut

Frets

Neck

Body

Pick guard

Pickups

Pickup
selector switch

Bridge

Volume &
tone controls

Plug (to amp.)

Vibrato arm

The Parts of a Guitar

work to "project" the sound out of an instrument that is not being aided by electric amplification. Some say this is a good argument for beginning on the acoustic before switching to the electric guitar, and I must admit that I, for the most part, agree. But if rock lead guitar is what inspires you in the first place, you should go right into it rather than be discouraged by the acoustic. Anyway, who says you can't pick up an acoustic at a later date, or learn on both at once! I went back to the acoustic several years after playing almost exclusively electric, and found that I had created my own unique approach to the acoustic guitar. Perhaps you'll find the same true for you!

The "playability" of your guitar is of the utmost importance, yet many players who are just starting out are really in the dark regarding such matters. This can be potentially devastating, as you can end up with a guitar that may be hopelessly troublesome, which can sometimes discourage you from playing at all!

There are important things to look for when checking out a guitar for its condition. The "action," or height of the strings, is crucial to playing comfort and can usually be adjusted without major expenditures.

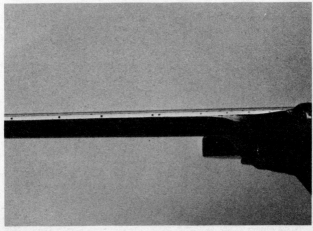

Seeing the guitar's "action" or string height from the sides

A guitar's action should neither be too low nor too high. There should be a bit of effort involved in creating the notes themselves, and I feel that this helps the overall sound and emotional scope of the musician's playing. Also, if the action is too low, as too many players prefer it, you'll have a difficult time trying to bend strings, as well as get too much string and fret "buzz." Action that is too high is quite easy to spot, you simply have a hard time pressing down the strings! Sometimes the strings can be so high that the notes are *sharp* when they are fretted! This is rare, though it does signal a really bad action problem. Most electric guitars have adjustable bridges (the string height can be raised or lowered), but when serious problems exist, this is only part of the solution. Neck warpage, or bowing, is often the culprit if there is a severe action problem. You can check the neck's straightness by eye, looking down the neck from the bridge or nut; placing a straightedge across all the frets can tell you where the warp is.

Looking down the neck to check for warpage or bowing

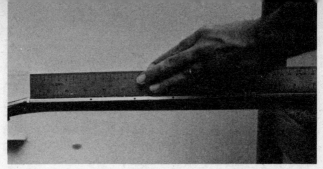

Placing a straight-edge over the frets to check straightness of the neck

Most modern electric guitars are equipped with an adjustable *truss rod*. This device, inside the length of the neck, is usually made of steel and serves to maintain the straightness of the neck. Most can be loosened or tightened, depending on what is required to get the neck properly set. On the Gibson-style guitars, the truss rod is usually adjusted at the headstock, where the end of the rod is covered by a small plate. Fender-style necks more often have the adjustment mechanism at the base of the neck.

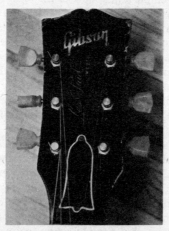

Gibson Les Paul headstock showing cover for the truss-rod adjustment

Note truss-rod adjustment screw at the base of the neck of
this Fender Stratocaster

If you are experiencing "action" problems and related
annoyances, such as string buzz, and the guitar's neck is
straight, then simple adjustment of the bridge is probably
all that's required. A bridge that enables you to raise and
lower each string individually is the most desirable and
is certainly prevalent on good guitars. These bridges are
usually adjusted by either a small screwdriver or an Allen
wrench. It should be pointed out here that Fender-style
necks are arched, while Gibson-style ones are flatter. This
means that when you adjust a Fender bridge, you must
maintain the arched angle of the fingerboard if you intend
to get an even action across all six strings.

As far as "action" is concerned, I generally believe in
keeping the strings high enough so that there is some
degree of effort behind the notes. I also enjoy "slide"
guitar playing, and if you intend, as I do, to "double" on
slide and regular playing on one guitar, you need to have
the action high enough to facilitate both techniques. Certainly, with action that's too low, you really can't expect
to have enough leverage for proper string bending or
vibrato. So we see that even though low action may *seem*

Note Fender-style bridge, with individual height adjustments for each string, and vibrato unit.

to make playing easier, it can really hamper some of the more physical and emotional aspects of guitar playing. Be sure to have your guitar set up the way it feels right for *you*!

Choosing the Right Guitar for You

These days, walking into the local music shop may be enough to start you daydreaming or may forever confuse you as to what a guitar even *looks* like! This is understandable, as there is an incredible selection available, and the choice of styles, woods, colors, sounds, weights, and so forth is unprecedented. It's particularly difficult to decide on the right guitar when you're just starting out. You may be first attracted to the one that looks "cool" to you, but as far as knowing what guitar is right for your style of playing?—*What* "style"?! This is, of course, where an experienced teacher or player can help a lot, and it would be advisable to have him or her come along on any guitar safari you may have planned. It's very important that the shape and circumference of the neck correspond to the shape of your hand and the length of your fingers. You must also make sure that the guitar feels right when you play it in both the standing and the seated positions. Many of today's flashier instruments are made with the guitarist's comfort last in mind, so beware. I am particularly opposed to instruments that are too heavy. I believe that they are a deterrent to the general well-being of the guitarist and can ultimately discourage him or her from even picking it up. The old adage that "heavier guitars have more sustain" just isn't true. It's really the lighter, more porous instruments that resonate more and offer better sustaining capabilities. The world-renowned Gibson Les Paul guitar can, however, be an exception. It is generally a heavier instrument than most but possesses fine playability and feels good to hold.

The guitar I really "cut my teeth" on as far as rock and roll and blues go is my gold-top 1952, one of the very first Les Pauls ever built. This guitar has single-coil P-90 pickups on it and is somewhat lighter than the later models, which have humbucking pickups, more hardware and often heavier woods on them. (Humbucking pickups cancel out extraneous electronic noises by using two magnetic coils of opposite polarities next to each other. Single-coil pickups, though clearer in tone, do sometimes have this noise problem.) Of course, my *very* first electric guitar was several years before that, and wasn't nearly as glamorous. It was a Japanese "Ideal;" a four-pickup monster that had more chrome on it than a '59 Cadillac! It really wasn't the right guitar for me to start out on, for it was very hard to play, but it served the purpose, and anyway, I got to meet Charlie Watts of The Rolling Stones, who was also

1952 Les Paul standard (Bridge unoriginal)

in the little shop when I was buying my first electric guitar! This was 1965, and the Stones were about to make their first New York appearance, and I was the only kid in the store who even recognized him! Perhaps the most incredible part of this story occurred when in 1985, twenty years later, I was telling the same story on a London radio show. Believe it or not, the road manager who was with Charlie Watts that very day phoned in to the station, and said he actually *remembered* me as the little boy in the shop who asked Charlie Watts for his autograph! Well, you can see that you'll never know *what* to expect when buying your first guitar! Who knows, maybe Eddie Van Halen will help you tune it up!?

The Les Paul, like many other classic guitars, has given birth to countless other models that try to capture its essence, both in appearance and sound. Some companies, such as the Japanese ESP and Tokai, mostly replicate the older classics, while a few of the American companies such as Guild and Kramer, present new variations on the theme.

Japanese-made ESP Navigator. A fine Les Paul look-alike

An advanced play upon the Les Paul theme, the Guild Nightbird actually has hollow sound chambers beneath the top.

The Fender Telecaster, first introduced in 1948 as the Broadcaster, was the first production solidbody sold, making it the father of solidbody electric guitars. Quite a few guitarists, yours truly included, feel that the makers got it right the first time! The "Tele," as many call it, is also a two-pickup instrument, possessing a more searing treble than the Les Paul, with a noticeably clearer, cleaner tone. It is also a comparatively lightweight instrument, with a flat, slab-style body, as opposed to the more sculpted Les Paul. Again, it's important to point out that these Fender-style guitars generally come with an arched, or curved, fingerboard, as opposed to the flat, rather wide Les Paul Gibson-style fingerboard. You may prefer one over the other, depending upon the length of your fingers, but either can be gotten used to. I find that I can be a bit more versatile on the rounded fingerboard and that I needn't play as "over" the frets on the Fender as I do on the Gibson. Be sure to experiment with both neck types before you decide which one best suits your hand.

The Telecaster has also been copied by other companies, and Fender itself has reissued a version of the original model they made famous so many years ago. Other companies, such as ESP, Kubicki, Yamaha, and Fernandes have all made good Tele-type guitars.

1953 Fender Telecaster

Two fine contemporary Telecaster look-alikes: A black ESP and a unique "Wildwood" Kubicki

The Fender Stratocaster was introduced in late 1953. It was the second design Fender released and is probably the most popular electric guitar of all time. Over the years, as in the case of the Telecaster, there has been barely a change made to this instrument, and it remains a true classic. The vintage Strats command some pretty hefty prices, while many of the same companies I have mentioned do make excellent "knock-offs."

A trio of vintage Fender "Strats" l-r: 1958, 1954, 1957

Brand new ESP strat copy; a fine, low-priced guitar

Fender's Stratocasters were among the first guitars to introduce a vibrato arm to the public, and as far as musical trends are concerned, this contraption has certainly stood the test of time. From the early days of simulating Hawaiian guitar sounds to the late-fifties and early-sixties surf sound, from the guitar acrobatics of Jimi Hendrix to today's screaming heavy metal sounds, the vibrato—or "whammy" bar, as it's often called—has indeed enjoyed a roller-coaster ride of popularity. One of the vibrato unit's major drawbacks has always been its tendency to put the guitar out of tune once it has been employed. This problem has finally been dealt with, though, as many manufacturers have begun making units with locking mechanisms that prevent tuning slippage. The two most prominent names in this field have been Floyd Rose and Kahler, while other makers are manufacturing variations upon their themes.

Kahler locking tremelo system installed on a Guild guitar

Heavy metal guitar's reemergence these days has given birth to some incredibly bold and inventive guitar designs. Some of these are quite functional, while others are merely ornamental. The original designs of the Gibson Flying V and Explorer have inspired some of the more popular takeoffs by companies such as Hamer, Aria, Washburn, Guild, and Ibanez, which have all played upon this flashy design theme in one way or another. It should be noted that the Explorer shape, though extreme in appearance, is exceptionally comfortable to play and has, in many ways, a perfectly balanced body for both standing and sitting. One of the early Gibson guitars that was a modification upon this design was the Firebird, made in the early sixties. The model I have pictured is a rare transitional one, with a reverse body and a *non*-reverse headstock, circa 1964.

A rare transitional Gibson Firebird. Early reverse body, later non-reverse headstock

Because the selection is quite large, I've only scratched the surface of today's guitar designs. The main idea is to find the guitar that is comfortable and appealing to *you*, rather than buy it as a result of a passing fancy for its appearance. These days, you really don't have to spend more than three to four hundred dollars for a guitar, such as an ESP or Guild, that will suit your needs for a long time to come. Be sure to make the salesman go through the paces, showing you all of the guitar's features, because guitar-shop salesmen are a notoriously impatient sort, with very little time for beginners. If you don't get the information you want, go elsewhere; there'll be someone who will steer you right. If you already *do* know what you want and price is the only object, you might do well to look for a used instrument and buy it from another guitarist, instead of a store, where it will be marked up anyway. Besides, it's sometimes easier to put a guitar through its paces in someone's house than in a crowded music store. Take your time when shopping for your guitar. This is a friend you'll be keeping with you, hopefully, for a long time.

In addition to this book, there are lots of publications out there that want to help you in choosing your instrument and making you a better player. *Guitar Player* magazine has really become the "Bible" for guitarists the world over and it has, for a very long time, contained columns and articles by some of the world's top artists (and by yours truly, as well), about equipment and playing. Other magazines that play upon the same theme are *Guitar World, Frets, Guitar for the Practicing Musician*, and *Circus*. These magazines all feature columns where the latest equipment is reviewed and evaluated, and with today's endless choices, they *can* make a difference.

I'm a true believer in going with the original designs if you're just starting out. I feel that within the Les Paul, Strat, and Tele styles you should be able to find your dream guitar, as well as have a guitar whose design has stood the test of time. If you desire some of the newer features, such as locking vibrato or different pickups, many new guitars now offer them as stock options; these options can also be installed in your existing instrument. Happy hunting!

Amplifiers

We've all seen the rock bands with stacks upon stacks of high-powered amplifiers behind them, able to reach ear-shattering levels of volume. However, did you know that in the recording studio, that sound is often achieved with something as small as a lunchbox? It's true, and you needn't have stacks of amps to get the sound you want during practice, or playing smaller-size clubs. As with guitars, today's amps offer the player far more versatility than the amps of days gone by, and there is an endless array of sizes, speaker configurations, and power ratings to choose from.

SMALL AMPS

I always find this kind of amplifier most intriguing, particularly because small amps can usually do more than their size indicates. There have been many tiny amps introduced over the years, with Fender once again leading the way, with its famous Champ Amp. These amps were designed strictly for practicing at home, but they can be very useful in the studio when you need an overdriven, distorted sound without breaking your back trying to carry the equipment in! Many of rock's greatest solos have been recorded using something not much bigger than these. Fender, Peavey, Guild, Music Man, and Yamaha all have fine tiny amps available today. I would highly recommend buying one of these models. Just be aware that you are getting an amp that is not suitable for *every* application.

These "small" amps usually contain one speaker with a diameter of either 6, 8, 10 or 12 inches, and they almost always have an *open* back. The Fender Deluxe Reverb has always been my trusty recording amp and can sound sweet and clean or distorted and overdriven. This kind of amp is extremely versatile and lends itself to more situations than the tiny practice amp.

The small but mighty Fender Champ Amp, late Fifties tweed-style

circa 1965 Fender Deluxe-Reverb

The Seymour Duncan Convertible Amp features various tube and transitor modules that can be snapped into the amp to achieve a wide variety of sounds. This is truly several different amps in one and is suited equally to live and studio situations.

The Seymour Duncan Convertible is a mid-sized amp offering infinite sound possibilities

MID-SIZED AMPLIFIERS

These are probably the most popular and versatile amps around and also represent the widest variety of power ratings and features. The Fender Twin-Reverb amp is one of the most popular mid-size amps of all time. With its high power rating and master volume control on later models it can put out a very clean sound as well as the classic overdriven tube sound. As is the case with many intermediate-size models, this amp contains two 12-inch speakers. Others, such as the well-known Super-Reverb, contain four 10-inch speakers, while still others may have one 15-inch or one 12-inch.

circa 1965 Fender Twin-Reverb

The mid-size amp, unlike its larger cousins, is the most versatile, and it's also easy to transport. I would suggest a model that contains *reverb* and, if possible, the feature of *channel switiching*. Provided the amp has two separate channels, this feature enables you to set two different tonalities, i.e. two distinct guitar sounds that can be activated by use of a foot switch. In this way, you can easily go from a rhythm sound to a lead sound, clean to dirty, etc.

There are so many amps on the market today that you'd be well advised to play through as many different models as possible before making a decision. Have the salesman review all the special features for you, and be sure to play through the amps at varying volumes. The level at which your speaker starts to distort, called "break-up," is crucial, and you'll want to know your amp's "threshold" before you purchase it. Not until you push your amp to this extreme will you know when it can handle no more volume.

LARGE AMPLIFIERS

If you're a beginning guitar player, the large amp may simultaneously be the most attractive yet least practical type for you to own. In live situations, the heavy metal artists and their founding fathers, such as Jimi Hendrix and Peter Townshend, always relied upon large stacks of huge amplifiers to get their "wall of sound" across. These amps, known as the "piggyback" style, usually come in two pieces. There are the speaker cabinet, usually consisting of four 12-inch speakers, and the amplifier section, or "head," which sits on top, separated from the speakers. One thing this type of rig really excells in is flexibility. You can add as many speaker bottoms as you wish or add more amp heads if you so desire. It is, of course, a lot to carry around with you to clubs, studios, and the like, and you rarely get a great sound out of these giants when playing softly. I can recall as a kid placing my piggyback amp facedown on the bed and cranking it up to ten so I could practice in my room! There is a multi-plicity of large, powerful amps on the market today, but some of the top names to try are Marshall, Boogie, Sey-mour Duncan, Hiwatt, Ampeg, Carvin, Yamaha, and Sunn. As with all the amps available on the market, I would strongly recommend the all-tube models as opposed to the transistor ones. Tubes will give you a more natural sound, and the tonalities of your guitar will come through much more colorfully.

You should try a large amp out, at least to live out your fantasies! However, these amps can be limiting to the beginner and are most useful in very large places, with

This Seymour Duncan is a fine example of a dual-stacked high-output amp

very loud bands. One day they may be just what you need; until then, stick with a smaller, more versatile amp— you'll be glad you did.

Your initial investment in your first amplifier needn't be more than $250 to $350. Companies such as Peavey,

Guild, Fender, and Roland manufacture many fine-quality lower-priced models. And if you keep the amp in good shape, it, like a guitar, will maintain good resale value when you intend to trade up to a higher-priced, more exotic model.

Chapter Two

STARTING TO PLAY

Now that you're relatively settled in with your equipment, we can begin the process of getting the right sounds out of your guitar. Even though many of you may already be playing somewhat by now, it would still benefit you to go over some of the fundamentals.

You must keep in mind the fact that even though we are dealing with fundamentals, these are some of the essential "building blocks" of guitar playing, and must be paid close attention to. In fact, they should be fun! Remember, the joy of playing the guitar isn't based upon *how much* you know but on *what* you know. Try to derive the most out of each step of the way, and the learning process should take shape nicely, becoming fun at the same time!

Proper Holding Positions

SITTING

When you are playing the electric guitar, it is usually customary to rest the instrument on your right leg, with both your feet on the ground. The most important thing to remember in this position is to balance the instrument in such a way that the left, or fretting, hand doesn't have to hold the guitar up. This would greatly inhibit your freedom of movement and your speed. Take note of how I'm holding it in the picture.

Proper seated position *(Deborah Roth)*

STANDING

This is, of course, the most popular form of playing the electric guitar and I believe quite necessary if you expect to really physically "get into" what you are playing. Again, it is crucial that you hold the guitar so that the left hand does not have to support it and is free to be totally at your command. The photo shows a very relaxed standing position, with the guitar strap set at the right length for me. You may prefer it higher or lower.

Proper standing position *(Deborah Roth)*

THE PICK

The flatpick, or plectrum, is an important tool for the rock guitarist. Where many forms of music don't necessarily require the sound of the pick, rock music, with its loud volume and hard hitting chords, can benefit directly from the use of a guitar pick.

Picks come in a seemingly endless array of shapes, sizes, and thicknesses, and these days many musicians are experimenting with exotic materials, such as stone and metal. For most applications, I prefer a medium-thickness pick, in a triangular shape, with two rounded sides. The photo shows a nice assortment of shapes and styles.

A selection of contemporary picks *(Deborah Roth)*

The proper right-hand picking position for rock guitar is also illustrated in a photo. The pick should be held between the thumb and forefinger, with a minimum of it exposed. In this way, you won't be gripping it too loosely or too tightly, and the pick will "give" slightly with each stroke. You should also be sure to hold your hand so the pick strikes each string at a similar angle: almost directly parallel to the strings themselves.

Proper position for holding the pick. Note how little of the pick is actually used *(Deborah Roth)*

The rock position of the left hand is exactly opposite to what is emphasized in classical and jazz training. Rather than having the hand arched high over the fretboard, with barely any opposing pressure applied by the thumb, the hand should be angled so the neck of the guitar fits snugly, almost like a baseball bat, through the palm. If your position is right, the strings should be cutting across the tips of your fingers at approximately a 45-degree angle.

The left hand "rock" position. Strings should intersect the fingertips at a 45° angle

Chord Checklist

Though I'm sure many of you now know a fair number of basic chords, I've provided here a diagram of several chords that you can refer back to as a reference guide or a learning tool.

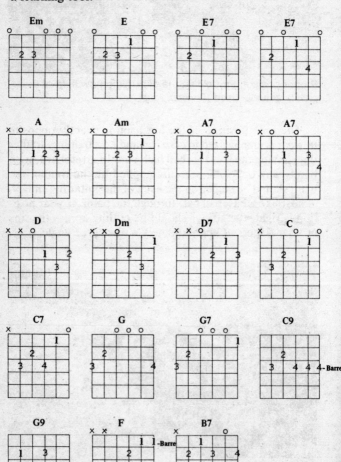

Explanation of Tablature and Special Symbols

For those who cannot read music and as an additional aid to those who can, I've provided guitar tablature below all of the standard notation in this book. The six horizontal lines represent the six strings of the guitar, with low E at the bottom:

A number intersected by the line represents the fret at which the left hand depresses the string. For example, here is how an open C chord would be shown:

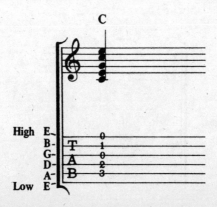

SYMBOLS

An arched line with an "S" over it tying two notes together means that there is a *slide* between the two notes. This will be used in the book to represent sliding with the finger. The slide symbol also means that only the first note is plucked, while the second is created by the slide itself:

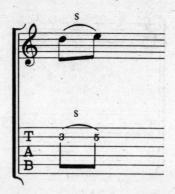

If the arch has an "h" over it, this illustrates a *hammer-on*. Here, the right hand picks only the first note. The second is sounded by "hammering-on" with a finger of the left hand higher up on the fingerboard:

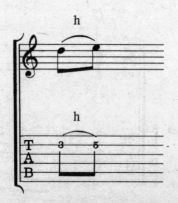

The same arch with a "P" over it represents a *pull-off*, or *left-hand pluck*. In this case, a note on a higher fret is plucked and then released (or "pulled-off"), leaving a lower-pitched note still sounding.

An arched line with a "B" over it represents a *bend*. A bend enables you to raise the pitch of the note by pushing or pulling the string toward or away from you at the same fret. Here, two notes are tied together; you play the first note, then bend that note to create the note that is in parentheses. Note that the bent note has a time value, just as the unbent note does:

An "R" signals a release of a bend. The usually occurs right after a bend, reversing the original action:

At times the release may occur alone. Here, the string is bent *before* it is picked:

A straight line pointing up or down *toward* a note means you slide *to* that note from an optional point below or above it. A straight line pointing up or down *away* from a note means you should slide *from* that note without sounding another specific note with the slide:

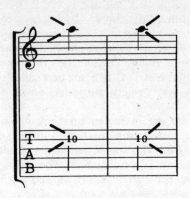

A note played with *vibrato* will have a wavy line over it. The proper technique of vibrato will be discussed later on in the book:

How to Tune the Guitar Properly

Before we get on with our playing, it's important that we be in proper tune and, in the process, learn to tune the instrument properly. Tuning properly is essential to good playing. If an instrument is out of tune with *itself*, it will invariably stick out like a sore thumb when combined with other instruments! Tuning is of course, a relative thing, like language. A Indian sitar, for example plays very different melodies and is therefore tuned differently from a guitar. The intervals that we tune on the Spanish guitar, E-A-D-G-B-E, are best suited to the scales and sounds that western music has adapted as its language.

First, to get the instrument on the way to being tuned, we must get a note from a reliable outside source, such as a recently tuned piano, a harmonica, a pitch pipe, an electronic tuner, or a tuning fork. The tuning fork is my usual choice, because it's easily transported in my guitar case and is perfectly consistent year after year. The most common tuning forks available on the market are A or E, which are both notes of open strings on the guitar. The E fork would probably be better for you to get, because there are two strings tuned to E on the guitar. Now, assuming you've matched the pitch of the low E string (the one closest to you) to the tuning fork, you can now tune the A string by pressing down the E string at the fifth fret and tuning the A string to match that tone. We can now tune the D string in the same manner—to the fifth fret on the A string. The G is tuned to the D string the same way, fifth fret to open G, but the B string is tuned differently. In this case alone, we must depress the *fourth* fret on the G string and then match the tone of the B string to *it*. To tune the high E string to the B we can now return to the regular "fifth fret is equal to the next string" style of tuning. Remember, *only* between the G and B strings do we tune from the fourth fret instead of the fifth.

TUNING WITH HARMONICS

Harmonics are very special bell-like tones that can be produced on certain frets of the guitar *without* pressing down the strings to the actual fret. This is achieved by lightly touching the string directly above the metal fret itself and releasing it a split second after the string has been plucked. This can occur with the best success at the twelfth, seventh, and fifth frets and can be an aid in tuning your guitar as accurately as possible. The photograph shows the proper position for creating a harmonic. Note the position of the finger directly over the fret itself.

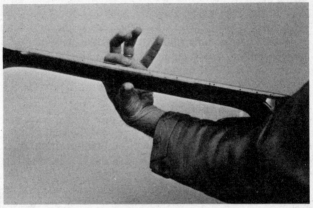

Touching a harmonic directly over the metal fret

Now, assuming that the low E is in tune, the harmonic you create at its fifth fret should be equal to the harmonic on the next string (A) at its seventh fret. This will bring out another of the advantages to this kind of tuning: you can sound both notes simultaneously while you tune them, which makes this much faster than the other method. You'll notice that if the pitches of the two strings differ, a wavering sound—or "beats," as it's often called—is produced. These beats will become longer and smoother-sounding the closer the pitches of the two strings are brought together, until there are no beats at all, when the strings are perfectly in tune.

The next two strings, the A and the D, are tuned in exactly the same manner—fifth fret harmonic to seventh fret harmonic—as are the next two, the D and G. The B string, that mischievous little fellow, once again puts a damper on things; another way of tuning is required, but it's not too bad. We must now go back to the low E string, sound the harmonic at the seventh fret, and match it to the *open* B string. The high E can be tuned to the B in the same fifth-fret-to-seventh manner, but the pitches are extremely high and make tuning a little more difficult than it need be. For this reason, I like to carry over the B-string style of tuning to the E, by sounding the seventh fret on the A string and simply matching it up with the open high E string. You should now be in the best tune possible. It may take you a while to get it right, but I believe the harmonic method of fine-tuning your instrument is far superior to the standard fretting style.

Fundamental Exercises

To get you used to the fingerboard and some alternating down-up picking, I've provided the open-position chromatic scale for you as a starter. In the chromatic scale

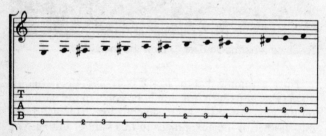

you move from one note to the next, without jumping any frets at all. You should work on maintaining a consistent position for both left and right hands, trying to achieve a similar angle of left-hand fretting and right-hand picking for each string. Start very slowly at first, and try to build up speed as your confidence and technique increase.

YOUR FIRST ROCK SCALE

First, I should explain just what "scale" is. When we play a particular scale, we are making a melodic decision to play only *certain* notes, usually in a pattern that involves these notes repeated over and over again. Hence, in a *pentatonic* scale pattern, or a scale involving five notes, the five notes can sometimes be repeated as many as four times in one scale run. After a while, when you've practiced the scales over and over, they tend to fall very naturally under your fingers and develop a "shape" that you can easily relate to on the fingerboard. It is then that the creation of licks from these scales can become much easier and more fluid.

There are many scale positions used in rock guitar, but none is so easily identified as the original basic-blues scale. This position, your first scale, is for the key of E and is in the "open" position. This means that a lot of open-string notes are included, and these open notes are a real guitarist's friend! I have it here in both music and diagram form. Try to play it ascending and descending and with alternating right-hand picking strokes, down-up-down-up.

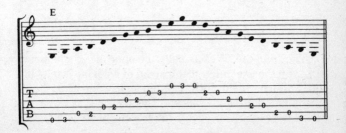

THE HAMMER-ON

One of the most useful tools a rock guitarist can have is the ability to play hammer-ons. This technique was initially discussed in the explanation of tablature and symbols section of the previous chapter. Please refer back to it should you need a more detailed description of the technique. This is one of the great techniques that enable you to play more than one note with only one stroke of the string. For this technique, try to have the hammering finger as close *above* the note to be hammered as possible, so as to have the highest degree of accuracy and strength within as small an area as possible. The fingers to be used in this exercise are easy to remember; second finger for the second fret, third finger for the third fret. Pluck each open string and then make the hammer-on above it. Try to hold down the hammered note for as long as its time value calls for. This will really make it sound as if you're giving "new life" to the string each time you hammer-on a note.

THE PULL-OFF

The "pull-off" is essentially the opposite of a hammer-on, with the exception that instead of its being just a "lift-off," which would not create enough volume, it should really be a left-hand "pluck." This means that when you want the pull-off to occur, the finger plucks downward, *away* from you, which gives the string a sound as if it were picked again. The pull-off very often occurs just after a hammer-on, and here we have the same open E blues scale utilizing a combined hammer and pull technique; first hammer-on and then pull-off the same note. Again, make sure the pull-off is *away* from you.

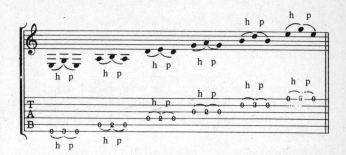

Of course, all positions on the guitar are not open ones, and hammer-on and pull-off techniques are very useful in closed positions where more than one finger is involved. First I would like you to practice this one-handed exercise, where just the left hand plays a repetition of hammer-ons and pull-offs. This is exactly how flashy guitarists "play with one hand," and the key is to maintain an even tempo to the notes and especially an even *volume*. This hammer-pull motion should be achieved with the index and middle fingers of the fretting hand. Be sure to anchor the index finger securely enough so as not to pull it out of tune when making the pull-off.

Now, here is the "closed" blues scale for the key of A.

We see it played here in the hammer-pull style I just described. Take note of the photo to see the position of the hand and finger just after the left-hand "pluck" has occurred.

The left hand, just after a 3rd finger "pull-off" has occurred
(Deborah Roth)

Chapter Three

THE ROCK GUITAR FAMILY TREE

In the "family tree" that I have diagrammed for you, I have simplified matters considerably. I've tried to limit the list to those guitarists who I feel are the most important, and although there can be countless categories, I feel that this grouping of musical styles best illustrates the make-up of rock guitar.

To help you gain more insight into the medium you are studying, the following are some short historical sketches of each category and the guitarists within them.

Early Blues Greats

The musicians in this category are truly the fathers of all rock music, for blues is the basis on which all later forms were developed. In the rural South, in states such as Mississippi, Louisiana, Texas, Tennessee, and Alabama, blacks developed their own unique folk music labeled "blues." The themes were often about the sadder,

THE ROCK GUITAR FAMILY TREE

EARLY BLUES GREATS

Mississippi John Hurt, Robert Johnson, Son House, Charlie Patton, Bukka White, Skip James, Willie McTell, Arthur Crudup, Willie Johnson, Fred McDowell

ROCKABILLY

Everly Brothers, Roy Orbison, Buddy Holly, Eddie Cochran, Carl Perkins, Elvis and Scotty Moore, Chet Atkins, Hank Garland, Duane Eddy, James Burton, Cliff Gallup, Jimmy Bryant

CHICAGO STYLE BLUES AND R&B

Howlin' Wolf, Albert Collins, Muddy Waters, Elmore James, Buddy Guy, Otis Rush, B.B. King, Bo Diddley, Chuck Berry, Albert King

LATER ROCK AND BLUES

Duane Allman, Roy Buchanan, Carlos Santana, The Beatles, The Rolling Stones, Eric Clapton, Jeff Beck, John Hammond, Jimmy Page, Leslie West, Jerry Garcia, Peter Townshend, Jimi Hendrix, Mike Bloomfield

JAZZ/ROCK FUSION

Carlos Santana, Jeff Beck, John McLaughlin, Larry Coryell, Pat Metheney, Larry Carlton, Steve Morse, Allan Holdsworth, Al Dimeola

HEAVY METAL

Ritchie Blackmore, Tony Iommi, Eddie Van Halen, Yngwie Malmsteen, Steve Vai, Gillis and Watson, Angus Young, Jay Jay French, Randy Rhoads, Gary Moore

CONTEMPORARY ROCK AND BLUES

George Thorogood, Stevie Ray Vaughn, Andy Summers, Brian Setzer, Dave Edmunds, Mark Knopfler more oppressive problems of life, hence the "blues" label, and a distinct "question-and-answer" form of lyrics and music became the best means of expressing these blues. This was strictly an acoustic form of music, involving fingerpicking and often "slide" guitar. Slide, or "bottleneck" guitar involves the use of a piece of metal, glass, or another similar object to create the notes on the guitar. It's usually worn over one of the fingers of the fretting hand, and can create some beautiful and haunting "vocal" sounds on the instrument. It's largely assumed that during the early twentieth century, the traveling minstrel shows that appeared throughout the South helped spread the idea of slide guitar to the rural blacks. They would often contain "exotic" Hawaiian dancers and musicians, and Hawaiian guitar is played with the guitar on the lap, face up, with a slide. The black players of the rural South would then recreate the sound by putting some metal tubing or a bottleneck over the finger, and would play the guitar in an upright position. Special "open" tunings were used for this style, in which the guitar was tuned to an open chord. You can hear the slide style incorporated into the music of almost every great early bluesman. Artists such as Robert Johnson, Son House, Charlie Patton, and Blind Willie Johnson all were deft slide players who combined this style with normal fretted playing to create a wide range of tones.

Of all the bluesmen to come out of the rural South, none could ever have had the impact that Robert Johnson did. He wrote some of the all-time blues classics, such as "Love in Vain," "Dust My Broom," "Crossroads Blues," and on and on. Many of these songs were later made into huge hits by such bands as The Rolling Stones ("Love in Vain"), and Cream ("Crossroads Blues"). His legacy was short, perhaps only twenty-nine songs or so, and he died so young, at around the age of twenty-four. Still, though, his blues is timeless, and the greatness of his music will live on forever. I must admit, it was pretty incredible being down in Mississippi shooting the film "Crossroads" thinking that some of those very roads may have been ones that Robert himself may have walked down! His playing directly influenced that of Muddy Waters and Elmore James, two bluesmen who left the South and helped pioneer the electric Chicago-blues sound.

There were so many great blues guitarists. Charlie Patton was perhaps the earliest and the first to make a name for himself through recordings, while Arthur Crudup's song, "That's Alright Mama" was actually Elvis Presley's first big hit. Son House claimed to have shown Robert Johnson a few tricks, as he well might have, and Bukka White inspired his cousin B. B. King to take up the guitar.

I strongly recommend that you go out and buy some records by these great early masters of the blues. This is where it all started, and you wouldn't even be considering playing the guitar today if it weren't for this great and rich tradition.

Chicago-Style Blues and R & B

As I started to indicate in my section on the early blues greats, Chicago was the next stop along the way in the historic travels of the blues. Many artists from the Mississippi delta and other Southern regions rich with music started to emigrate north to Chicago, where on the famed Southside, an entirely new blues tradition was formed. Musicians such as Elmore James, Muddy Waters, Little Walter (harmonica), Tampa Red, and later artists such as Buddy Guy and Otis Rush were to take the rural blues, electrify and amplify it, and make it into a larger more aggressive band-oriented form of music. The pulse of city life was now a part of the blues experience, and it's expression came through loud and clear on electric instruments. Elmore James scored a major hit with his stinging slide-guitar rendition of Robert Johnson's classic, "Dust My Broom," while Muddy Waters and the bassist Willie Dixon were to write and perform such classics as "I'm a Man" and "Seventh Son." There was an extremely active club scene in the southside of Chicago during the fifties and early sixties, and so much raw talent that even today it's hard to believe! Chuck Berry was turning out hit after hit on Chicago's Chess Records label, and was truly inventing rock and roll at the same time! Easily the greatest rock and roll songwriter/performer of the fifties, Chuck Berry is truly the father of rock and roll. His aggressive and fresh way of approaching the guitar is still enlightening guitarists everywhere, and of course, where would we all be if not for his classics such as "Johnny B. Goode," "Roll Over Beethoven," "Oh Carol," "Sweet Little Sixteen," "Living in the USA," "Rock and Roll Music," "Route 66," and countless others?! His influence was directly felt in the music of The Beatles and The Rolling Stones, and both groups recorded several of his classic songs. Bo Diddley was also a Chess Records artist, and his unique, hard-driving rhythm guitar style on hits such as "Mona" and "Bo Diddley" also helped shape and influence all of rock and roll.

Perhaps no guitarist has had as much of an effect upon blues lead guitar as has B. B. King. B.B. came from Mississippi, too, but rather than settling into the Chicago scene, his blues found a home in Memphis. A man of unbelievable stamina, he has toured constantly for at least thirty years, and is truly an international star. His playing had a direct influence on people like Eric Clapton, Mike Bloomfield, Buddy Guy, and almost any other latter-day blues player you can think of. Perhaps most distinctive is his incredible vibrato (a style discussed later in the book), and his unique phrasing. If you're at all going to know where rock guitar really comes from, please be sure to pick up some B. B. King albums.

Albert King, also a native of Indianola, Mississippi, where B.B. came from, has also had a substantial effect on the blues and rock guitar movements. He possesses a powerful, emotional style with incredible vibrato and attack. Still performing and touring, his influence is strongly felt in the playing of Billy Gibbons, Eric Clapton, and Jeff Beck.

Through artists like Buddy Guy, Albert Collins, and Otis Rush, the Chicago Blues tradition is still alive and well, though it'll never be like the late fifties. It's important that we go out and see these performers and catch some of the tradition before it fades away entirely. Hopefully, it never will.

Rockabilly

In the mid-fifties, there were a select group of white recording artists who were taking their country and gospel roots, mixing them up with the black blues sounds, and coming up with a whole new trend called rockabilly. This was perhaps the first great transition made to really create rock and roll, for it finally broke down some of the racial barriers that were and still are common to music. At Sun Records, a small label in Memphis, Tennessee, a man named Sam Phillips was making musical history. At one time, his roster of artists included Elvis Presley, Carl Perkins, Johnny Cash, Jerry Lee Lewis, and Roy Orbison! All this on a tiny, independent label in Memphis! Rockabilly was of course not strictly confined to Memphis, as there were other stars such as Buddy Holly, Eddie Cochran, and Gene Vincent and the Bluecaps from all parts of the country. The rockabilly sound was perhaps the most important in introducing rock and roll to England, and guitarists like Duane Eddy, James Burton (with Rick Nelson), Buddy Holly, and Cliff Gallup (with Gene Vincent) all toured there and turned on an entire new generation; a generation of English guitarists who were to make Americans sit up and take notice of what they've had all along, but were too fickle to be aware of. Needless to say, when The Beatles recorded some of Carl Perkin's classics such as "Honey Don't" and "Matchbox," George Harrison was sure to replicate Perkin's guitar parts note for note. James Burton, who spent years playing with Ricky Nelson, and later with Elvis, is widely considered the first and most influential Telecaster player in rockabilly. The Telecaster "elite" group consists of players such as Roy Buchanan, Roy Nichols, James Burton, Albert Lee, and these are all hot pickers indeed! Scotty Moore was a big influence and he played all of the lead on the early Elvis recordings. A very inventive player, his distinctive soloing can be heard on songs such as "Jailhouse Rock," and "Houndog

Blues." Perhaps most interesting was Cliff Gallup's work with Gene Vincent. This was a rockabilly player of such inventiveness, that his solos are *still* difficult to pick up off the record! He was only with Gene Vincent and the Bluecaps for a short time, but his influence is still deeply felt. Albert Lee and Brian Setzer, rockabilly revivalist with The Stray Cats, both cite him as a prime influence.

Thanks to groups such as The Stray Cats and artists like Dave Edmunds, rockabilly has been enjoying a big upsurge in popularity lately. It's important that it remains a recognized and important American musical form, rather than merely the "fashion" that so many people mistake it for. The period during which both white rockabilly and black R&B ala Chuck Berry was being created was probably the richest and most creative musical time for the then embryonic rock and roll, and it's a period well worth studying!

Later Rock and Blues

This is perhaps the most generalized category, and represents the broadest scope both in style and time frame. When I refer to this as "later rock and blues," I basically mean the period that followed and included The Beatles and the whole British "invasion" of the early to mid-sixties. These are the artists who brought back the blues, rockabilly, and other American forms of music, while at the same time creating a whole new sound and energy that was to influence an entire generation.

The premier trendsetter from the U.S. during this period was without question Michael Bloomfield. His work with the Paul Butterfield Blues Band and with Bob Dylan represents some of the most electrifying lead guitar ever, and he was largely responsible for creating a blues "boom" in the late sixties. In fact, which *guitar* he played was as important to others as what he played *on* it. It seemed that when he switched to a sunburst Les Paul, so did Clapton, Page, Beck, and all the other British blues/rockers. In fact these guitars are still among the most highly prized collector's items to be found anywhere. Eric Clapton, through his work with John Mayall, Cream, Blind Faith, and Derek and the Dominoes, was holding down the British blues throne, while Jimmy Page was pushing the idiom more to the heavy metal sounds we're so familiar with today. Jeff Beck, another legendary British player, was among the first to extend the guitar's sonic limits, with feedback, fuzztones, wah-wahs, etc., and also began an early venture into the realm of the jazz/rock fusion sound. One unique little part of British rock guitar history is that Clapton, Beck, and Page *all* played with the Yardbirds within a very short time of each other, and they *all* went on to incredible fame. Beck did a lot of work with Rod Stewart, and in fact, Rod Stewart was the singer in Beck's band in the early seventies. As of late, they've collaborated again, and Beck had a memorable solo on Stewart's recent hit, "People Get Ready." Jimmy Page formed Led Zeppelin and was at the helm of that pioneering metal band for it's entire life. These days, he has a band called The Firm, a group that he formed with Paul Rodgers, the respected British singer from the band Bad Company. Jerry Garcia for years has had a hold on his own brand of west-coast blues/rock guitar with The Grateful Dead, and of course, Keith Richards continues to reshape and reinvent Chuck Berry with The Rolling Stones. Pete Townshend, the guitarist from The Who for so many years who is now on his own, developed a unique and dynamic lead/rhythm style that occasionally included the technique of smashing the guitar into the amp and splintering it in a hundred pieces! (This technique is strictly optional for the student!) Duane Allman and The Allman Brothers Band helped create a new form of Southern Rock, and along with Dickie Betts, they created a new and often imitated double-lead guitar style that incorporated much two part harmony work. Duane was also an exceptional blues player, and his slide playing was among the most innovative and melodic of all time.

There are countless great guitarists who made their mark during the sixties and early seventies, but none looms over the crowd so prominently as does Jimi Hendrix. During the late sixties, this guitarist was literally creating a one-man revolution on his instrument. And in the thick pack of players who were around in those days, that was almost an impossible thing to do. He was able to successfully bridge the gap between psychedelia and true emotion with a use of sounds and innovations that remain unmatched even today. Hendrix came from deep blues and R&B roots, and this soulfulness was very effectively communicated through his playing. In the year before he died, he began to play more straight blues, casting off much of the psychedelic showiness and flash for a subtler, perhaps more somber and expressive form of guitar. Whatever he *did* play, though, he left an incredible legacy for all of us to benefit from. It's scary to think of what he could have accomplished had he not suffered such an untimely death. Listen to lots of Hendrix, and you'll hear what most of today's guitar heroes are trying to achieve!

Heavy Metal

Heavy metal guitar was really a form that developed in the late sixties from people simply playing very *loud* blues. In those days, players such as Leslie West, Jimmy Page, and Jeff Beck were at the forefront, but heavy metal as a musical form did not enjoy much more than a few years or so of popularity. Of course now, in the eighties, heavy metal has returned with a vengeance, so much so that it is in itself, a fairly broad musical field.

The players who are popular in metal—and there are many—seem to come in two types. You either have the technical-wizard types like Eddie Van Halen or Yngwie Malmsteen for instance, or the more emotional, blues-based types such as Gary Moore, Ritchie Blackmore, and Brad Gillis. One thing is for sure, however, and that is that *all* of them play *loud*, *very* loud.

In the most simple sense, heavy metal guitar is first characterized by fat-sounding "power" chords. These rarely contain the third of the chord, instead they almost always consist of the root and fifth—these terms are covered in more detail on page 00. Lines are often played in unison with the bass player, and the singer rarely goes below a primal scream. Seriously, though, this can be an interesting form of music, and it has it's roots deep in the blues and early rock. The technical virtuosity of some of the metal players today has really started to reach the outer limits, and in fact, if you listen to the playing of wizards such as Steve Vai and Yngwie Malmsteen, you'll hear as much Paganini and Bach as you would Clapton and Page!

Unfortunately, there are a lot of almost "generic" heavy metal bands floating around out there that contain guitarists with little to offer. That's not as out of the ordinary as the fact that many kids today think that lead guitar consists of nothing but the flash and sameness that these guitarists possess. This is why I feel that if you're into heavy metal, and if you're reading this book you just might be, please go to the source. Don't only listen to Angus Young of AC/DC, listen to who *he* listened to, and on and on. Your playing can only benefit from this knowledge, and you'll be guaranteed more longevity in the business than 90 percent of the heavy metal musicians out there making it today!

Jazz/Rock Fusion

The fusion of jazz and rock styles was inevitable. As techniques got more complex and tastes more demanding, many guitarists wanted to look beyond the usual pentatonic and blues scale sounds to more exotic and experimental forms of expression. Even well-known blues and rock players such as Carlos Santana and Jeff Beck started to work within the fusion medium back in the midseventies, and at the forefront of this new style was and still is, the masterful John McLaughlin. McLaughlin took the guitar world by storm when he and his band, the Mahavishnu Orchestra released the album "The Inner Mounting Flame" around 1970. For the first time, rock guitar fans were treated to a barrage of notes unlike they'd ever heard before, and barely with a hammer-on or a pulloff! In the fusion style, almost every note is picked, and that combined with the sustain and loud volume of the music can create some truly remarkable effects. Players such as McLaughlin, Al DiMeola and Steve Morse all possess incredible right-hand picking technique, and the speed at which they can play is nothing short of blinding! Remember, though, speed is impressive, but far from everything!

Much of this fascinating form of music is being played on acoustic guitar these days, and if you listen to the records of people like Larry Coryell, Al DiMeola, McLaughlin or even Larry Carlton, you'll note that there is a definite movement toward the acoustic guitar in fusion.

It also must be pointed out that a lot of the technical virtuosity found in fusion guitar has helped change the way heavy metal players approach their instruments, and there has been more than a bit of overlapping within the two styles as of late.

For the rock fan, this kind of playing can sometimes be hard to bear, and listening to fusion for many is an acquired taste. Still, it's a very important style to be aware of, and if you get hip to it, it just might change your playing forever.

Contemporary Rock and Blues Guitar

This again is a very broad field of players, but let's say it includes everyone but current heavy metal, jazz, and fusion players! Rock is becoming even more eclectic, and even the fact that we can now have so many sub-categories within it indicates the incredible variety of sounds being made.

There are, of course, the blues-revivalists, such as George Thorogood and Stevie Ray Vaughn who are white, third-generation players. These relative newcomers on the blues scene are exciting, and hopefully will encourage tomorrow's rock guitarists to go back to the source—the early blues greats.

Rockabilly has enjoyed quite a revival at the hands of some pretty impressive players such as Brian Setzer (with The Stray Cats) and Dave Edmunds. This phenomenon, too, particularly in the case of Setzer, has awakened the masses to some of the rootsy sounds of the fifties. Still, the music is fresh, and most of all it is saying something the people want to hear.

Andy Summers, with the truly distinctive band, The Police, helped define and refine new-wave rock guitar, with his abandonment of long solos for a more textural, percussive way of approaching the guitar. He also revolutionized the role of the guitar within a three-man situation, by contributing more to the overall than simply being the frontman. Clearly an important guitarist! Though a great soloist in his own right, Mark Knopfler, of Dire Straits has lately let his solos step out of the limelight as well, in favor of the songs themselves. Though his guitar parts to both "Sultans of Swing" and "Money for Nothing" are both classics, they are as different as night and day in approach.

This seems to be the stuff that contemporary rock guitar is made of today—eclecticism and a commitment to the *song* first, the licks and the solos last. This doesn't mean you should hang up your hot licks; it just means that modern rock is more than just a slick riff or a flashy lead. It can be a lot of fun, but it's serious business, too!

Chapter Four

THE MUSICAL ROOTS OF ROCK GUITAR

When one studies any style of contemporary music, it is essential that he or she become acquainted with the *roots* of what he or she is playing. In no musical form is this more apparent than in rock music, for it has enjoyed such a fast and tumultuous evolution that one can get caught up in at least ten different mini-eras as the "roots of rock"!

The real roots of rock guitar lie in blues music. First there was rural acoustic blues, exemplified by the sounds of the Mississippi delta region. Then the blues moved to northern cities, like Chicago, and became louder, amplified, electrified, and more band-oriented. This brought in instruments such as drums and bass, and with this development, rock 'n' roll was not far behind. Urban blues masters, such as Chuck Berry and Bo Diddley, began to take the blues format and make it a bit more up-tempo and melodic, moving more into the "rhythm and blues" category, while at the same time white musicians, such as Elvis Presley, Carl Perkins, and Jerry Lee Lewis, were creating rockabilly—a form of rock and roll that bridged rural country sounds with the black blues and R&B that they loved so much. This was the beginning of rock and roll, and out of this period came some of the hottest guitar playing the world has ever known.

Throughout the blues and this new rhythm and blues music, the I–IV–V twelve-bar blues pattern was the major format by which songs were written and to this day is the basis of all rock and roll and jazz music. Here is how this well-known pattern looks on paper.

I   I⁷

| / / / / | / / / / | / / / / | / / / / |

IV   I

| / / / / | / / / / | / / / / | / / / / |

V   IV   I   V

| / / / / | / / / / | / / / / | / / / / |

The Shuffle Pattern

One of the most popular ways to play blues or rock and roll progressions is in the form of the "shuffle." If you can imagine it, the four beats of the measure can be divided into triplets; in other words, three notes to every beat. Now, in the shuffle, we take each triplet and divide it into two notes, one a bit longer in duration than the other. This gives the shuffle a jaunty feeling, rather than a succession of monotonous eighth notes that all sound the same.

The shuffle position is an easy one, because it generally consists of the two bottommost notes of a chord, particularly if they're the root and fifth. The root is the same note as the key you are in, therefore it's referred to as the "root" of the chord. The fifth is another note contained in the root chord that is *five* notes away in the major scale of that key. For example, if the key or root is A, the fifth is E. Here are some open and closed positions of the shuffle lick for a variety of chords. In the case of the open position, we play the note with the index finger; in the closed positions, the ones without any open strings we play with the index and ring fingers.

As it is played, the shuffle pattern has a very catchy whole-step (two-fret) jump as part of the lick. Play each part of the lick twice, and this time, play it with *all* down-strokes. Remember, we are now playing *two* strings at once, as opposed to one.

This shuffle pattern involves only the two lowest strings of the chord, maintaining the same fundamental position for the E, A, and B chords. When playing the closed position, anchor the first and third fingers while making the extended note a stretch with the pinky. Good luck with it!

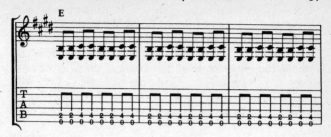

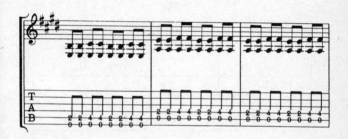

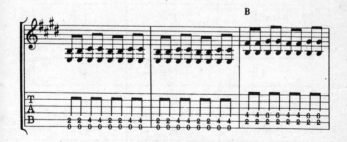

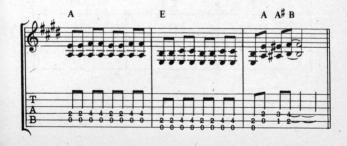

So that you can experiment and learn, here is a chart listing all the keys and their IV and V chords. These are the chords that would apply to this progression in any key. The IV is always three whole notes away from the tonic in the *major* scale of that key, and the V is the next note. The tonic is very simply the base note of the key in which you are playing. For example, if you are playing in the key of E the tonic note would be E.

I (Tonic)	IV (Sub-dominant)	V (Dominant)
E	A	B
F	A♯	C
F♯	B	C♯
G	C	D
G♯	C♯	D♯
A	D	E
A♯	D♯	F
B	E	F♯
C	F	G
C♯	F♯	G♯
D	G	A
D♯	G♯	A♯

Chuck Berry *(Ebet Roberts)*

This pattern brings to mind the playing of the father of rock and roll guitar, Chuck Berry. He is certainly the most inventive and important rock guitarist of the fifties, and his style of both rhythm and lead playing has influenced the entire scope of rock guitar since he started, back in the mid-fifties. Without him, there would be no Beatles or Stones, or anyone! I certainly recommend that you pick up some of Chuck's records to hear his inimitable style, not to mention some of the greatest rock and roll songs ever written! You'll certainly recognize the influence I'm talking about.

Songs such as "Johnny B. Goode," "Roll Over Beethoven," "Rock and Roll Music," "Sweet Little Sixteen," and countless others represent Chuck's finest hour, and

The author (left) performing with guitar legend Duane Eddy *(Deborah Roth)*

been one of my heroes, and recently I had the pleasure of meeting him backstage at New Jersey's Meadowlands while I was playing there with another rock guitar legend, Duane Eddy. What a thrill to shake Chuck Berry's hand!

Chuck always plays rhythm with shuffle licks, and he makes some enormous stretches to get them. This shuffle pattern in G shows the kind of stretching that is required

when playing in all "closed" positions, such as this. Your hand will have to pivot off of the back of the neck so as to achieve the proper angle for the highest note of the shuffle lick, played by the pinky.

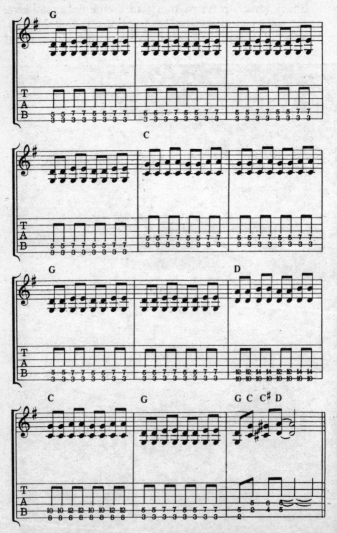

These shuffle positions are based upon something you've probably already heard about—barre chords. A barre means you use a finger to depress two or more strings at the same fret at the same time. This enables you to have much greater flexibility in terms of shifting chord positions. The two basic forms of the barre chord are the E and the A forms. In the shuffle, we are playing the two bottommost notes of the barre chord, though our barre with the first finger is no longer required. Our first finger should, however, lie lightly across the other strings to damp out any unwanted overtones or accidental notes that might occur in the act of playing.

There are two photos to illustrate the E and A forms of the barre chord. Note that in the A form we are only barring across the top *five* strings, as opposed to the six needed for the E form. It also should be mentioned that the index finger needn't press down all the strings, something that would be too painful to maintain for long periods of time; rather, it should curl around and let the boney side catch just the notes that must be played by the barre. In the case of the E form, these are the high E, B, and low E strings. In the A form, the strings played by the barre are only the A and high E. Take careful note of this "curled" position of my index finger in the two photos.

The E-Form barre chord *(Deborah Roth)*

The A-Form barre chord, covering only 5 strings *(Deborah Roth)*

These barre chords enable you to move up the neck and play different chords with the same positions. This chart clearly shows all the chords you can play with the E form barre, starting with the F chord at the first fret. When we reach the twelfth fret we are at another octave, so the pattern begins all over again.

The A form barre will afford you the luxury of these chords at each fret. Remember to barre only across the top *five* strings.

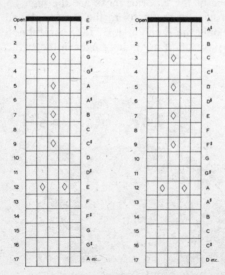

Open	E		Open	A
1	F		1	A♯
2	F♯		2	B
3 ◇	G		3 ◇	C
4	G♯		4	C♯
5 ◇	A		5 ◇	D
6	A♯		6	D♯
7 ◇	B		7 ◇	E
8	C		8	F
9 ◇	C♯		9 ◇	F♯
10	D		10	G
11	D♯		11	G♯
12 ◇ ◇	E		12 ◇ ◇	A
13	F		13	A♯
14	F♯		14	B
15	G		15	C
16	G♯		16	C♯
17	A etc.		17	D etc.

These barre forms can also be played as *seventh* chords, a sound closely related with blues and rock music. The seventh is simply the note that lies one full step (two frets) below the root note of the chord. The root note is the same as the tonic note; the root note of an E chord is the E note. The open positions are on the chord chart I gave you a few pages earlier, but here are the positions for both the E form and A form seventh chord barres. Note that in the case of the E form we have two options, one with a lower seventh, and one with two sevenths in it.

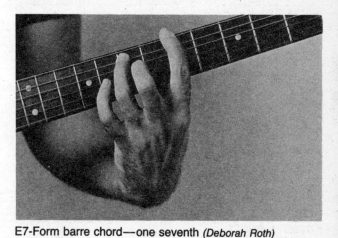

E7-Form barre chord—one seventh *(Deborah Roth)*

E7-Form barre chord with 2 sevenths in it *(Deborah Roth)*

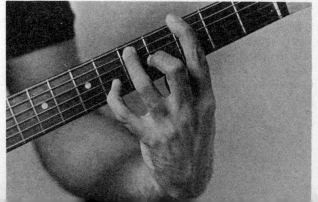

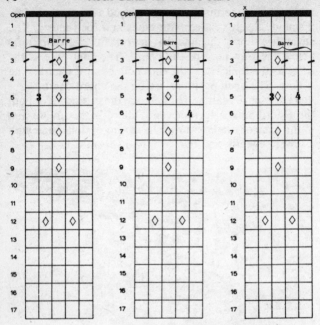

Power Chords

Power chords are generally associated with the harder-hitting forms of rock guitar, such as heavy metal and punk rock, but they owe their origin to the shuffle chord positions we were discussing in the last section. Power chords rarely contain the third of the chord, be it minor or major, hence making them *modal* in nature. In fact, being modal means they are not really chords at all—merely two-note harmonies. In the open positions these chords can be either two-note, as in the beginning positions of the shuffles, or contain a higher octave of the root as well, by the use of a "partial" barre. Here are the two open power chord positions for both E and A, using an index-finger partial barre that covers two strings at a time.

Open E power chord. Note how index finger also serves to damp out the high strings *(Deborah Roth)*

Open A power chord position *(Deborah Roth)*

If you wish to play modal power chords in the closed positions, simply base them upon the shuffle positions you are already familiar with. If you also wish them to become three notes, play them with your index, third, and fourth fingers. No barre is really necessary within the closed power chord positions.

These positions are very movable and flexible, and they have been the basis for many a hit song. Dave Davies, one of the founding members of the legendary British rock band The Kinks, helped give birth to the heavy-metal power chord sound with his rhythm guitar licks to such early hits as "You Really Got Me," and "All Day and All of the Night." These chord positions gave the songs an incredible "punch" and became among the most memorable guitar parts of the 1960s.

Here first, in the style of Dave Davies, is the "You Really Got Me" lick. It is rather simple in sound, but does require some fairly quick and accurate movement on the part of the left hand. You must play the chords firmly and cleanly but be able to abandon the fret quickly to move on to the next chord.

The lick to "All Day and All of the Night" has a similar approach but is a bit more difficult, since it uses more chords and movement. Practice it slowly at first, so as to not overshoot the frets you are sliding to.

The picture shows you the proper position for these closed two-note power chords. Note that though the index finger does not barre all of the strings, it still lightly touches them for damping purposes. Be sure to achieve the same angle as in the photo.

Closed power chord position for G

Suspended Chords

The use of *suspensions* within chords has been an important technique in rock guitar since it was first widely used by such innovative mid-sixties bands as The Byrds and The Beatles. Suspensions basically mean that there is a new note added on top of the original chord that alters it melodically and structurally. The most common suspended chords are the suspended fourth and second, while at times entire new chords are suspended on top of an existing bass note. Here are some diagrams illustrating some of the most widely used suspended positions. Make sure to play them with the original chord's position in mind.

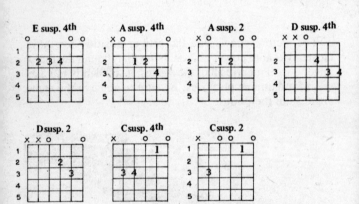

This little progression contains perhaps the most commonly heard suspended licks of the sixties. It's based mostly upon the folk/rock sound of The Byrds but was also used by The Beatles and has enjoyed a big resurgence in the New Wave sound. Songs such as "Mr. Tambourine Man" and "I'll Feel a Whole Lot Better" were Byrds classics that illustrated Roger McGuinn's unique suspended chords. George Harrison, of The Beatles, used this same approach on songs such as "I Need You," "Ticket to Ride," and "I Feel Fine." Many of the New Wave bands such as Tom Petty and the Heartbreakers, The Plimsouls, The Pretenders, and even The Police, have taken this idea directly from The Byrds and The Beatles.

Open D is also a very usable position for this lick. Be sure to arch your fingers high to allow the second and fourth fingers some room in this rather crowded little chord!

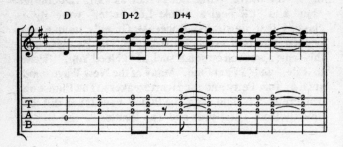

One of my own personal favorite power chord suspensions has the C form chord laid over the barred A form. This is an eminently usable position, and can be subtle and beautiful or loud and nasty. We have it here going from the open A position, again played with a partial index finger barre, with the partial C form then laid right over it but allowing the A bass note to ring.

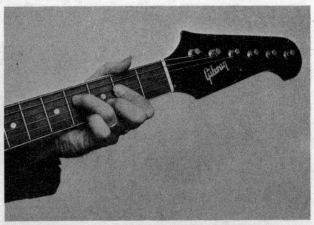

D chord over A. Note index finger barre for A chord

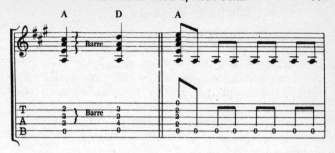

Peter Townshend of the Who *(Ebet Roberts)*

Peter Townshend's Power Suspensions

For over two decades, Pete Townshend was the driving force behind one of the most important rock groups in history, The Who. His style was unique, in the sense that he was a "lead rhythm guitarist." Single-note work rarely entered into his playing, but his rhythmic approach was so unique and dynamic that it became a lasting trademark. Though The Who have now disbanded, Pete continues a very active solo career and is still breaking new and exciting ground in rock music.

Peter Townshend is a true master of this style of rock guitar playing, and in fact, The Who's music has always relied heavily upon his use of suspended chords. One easily identifiable feature of his playing is his use of constant bass notes to add a sense of drama to the lick. This, along with occasional right-hand flourishes and slams, really makes him a "lead" *rhythm* guitarist! This exercise shows his approach to a constant bass rhythm part that contains both an A susp. 4th and an A susp. 2nd. Make sure to let the open strings ring cleanly, and be accurate with the constant bass.

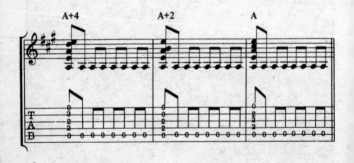

Townshend's distinctive right-hand flourishes became one of his trademarks as well, and they add intensity to the already intriguing sound of his suspended chords. This exercise combines them with the constant bass notes we played in the previous piece. Try to execute the flourishes and end them on time, landing right on the beginning note of the next constant bass pattern. The right-hand pattern for the flourishes is always down-up-down.

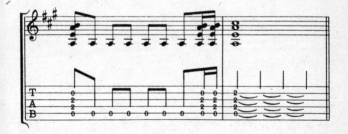

The C form chord on top of the A barre we discussed earlier also found its way into Townshend's playing, as well as that of countless other guitarists, and still remains a vital part of today's sound. Here we see a very innovative use of the pattern as it moves up and down the fingerboard. In this case, the open A frees the left hand to move all over, while the bass is kept as a constant foundation and reminder of the tonic. Note the tension that is deliberately created by some of the chords juxtaposed against the constant A bass note. Try playing this piece with the tension intended, with a very strong right-hand attack.

This fingerboard format has been very important to the music of The Rolling Stones over the years, and though often played in open G or A tuning by Keith Richards, these same rhythm parts can be done in standard tuning. Here are some recognizable variations on memorable Stones rhythm guitar parts, in the style of Keith Richards.

Keith Richards' Nasty Rhythm

Keith Richards of The Rolling Stones *(Ebet Roberts)*

Keith Richards is the quintessential rock guitarist. He borrowed directly from the early blues greats, such as Robert Johnson and Muddy Waters, mixed it up with a lot of Chuck Berry, and came out with The Rolling Stones' sound; raw and beautiful at the same time. Though much of the fancy guitar work on early Stones material was played by the late Brian Jones, you can pick out Keith's driving Chuck Berry–like licks in almost every song. His guitar playing is still the heart and soul of The Rolling Stones' sound, and I would strongly advise picking up *any* of their records to hear some truly great rock 'n' roll guitar!

Here is a prime example of Richard's unique rhythm guitar style.

Jimmy Page's Metal Led

Jimmy Page of Led Zeppelin and The Firm, playing his legendary Gibson double-neck *(Ebet Roberts)*

Jimmy Page is one of English rock's legends, and his style has proven to be one of the most influential around, particularly on the later heavy-metal sound. He started as a successful session player and was featured on many of The Kinks' early recordings. He was also one of the original members of The Yardbirds, a band that helped launch Eric Clapton and Jeff Beck as well. In the late sixties he formed Led Zeppelin, and his lead work with that band on songs such as "Whole Lotta Love" and "Stairway to Heaven" is truly classic material. Almost every heavy-metal great today would attest to Jimmy's powerful influence over them.

Heel damping the strings—using the heel of the right hand to mute unwanted sounds—which creates a duller, chunkier sound on the bass notes, in particular has always been a trademark of hard rock guitar, and the seminal Led Zeppelin records of the late sixties showcased some exemplary work by Jimmy Page using this technique. Page's approach is, in general, a crisp blend of lead and rhythm techniques, all closely coordinated with the bass line. This raw, blues-based style has given rise to many of the heavy-metal sounds we hear today. The heel-damp position is illustrated for you in the photo section. Be sure to cover the bottom three strings only and not to damp too far ahead of the bridge. This will render the notes barely audible, as well as make them too sharp.

Note placement of right hand for damping sound, just ahead of the bridge

Jimi Hendrix

Jimi Hendrix, a total guitarist, and one who forever changed the way we even look at a guitar, had a very unique power chord approach. He liked chords, and seemed to have a knack for breaking them up into bass and lead parts that would become hooks for some of his most famous songs. The "Foxy Lady" riff shows him at his best, playing fat bass notes along with the bassist, then throwing in some dissonant high chords as answers. He would then end with power lines again played in unison with the bass player. The chord we will be playing here is a new one, an E7#9, and it resembles our B7 position. Though it's odd-sounding, it's really quite easy to master and makes a good part of the hard rocker's repertoire.

The E7 barre chord position is also very useful in the Hendrix style and can achieve the same bass-and-lead note separation, only within a "closed" position. In this

case, we employ the seventh barre, which includes the high seventh on the B string, played by our pinky. Since this lick has an almost "question-and-answer" sound to it, you needn't press down the full chord until you're about to play it.

Classic Rock Chord Progressions

Over the years there have been certain progressions of chords that have become a permanent part of rock music. They are archetypal, and come up in jam sessions as often as they do in songs. A working knowledge of the classic chord progressions will help you in your improvisation and give you a "vocabulary" to work with when practicing or jamming.

This power chord progression found its way into the music of countless groups during the sixties and is still showing up quite a bit in heavy metal. There are many ways of dividing it up, but this particular way of playing it, with two beats of rest for each measure, lends itself well to the two-note power chord style.

This I-IV-V progression takes its roots from Latin music such as "La Bamba" and "Guantanamera," but of course is used in a heavier way here. Songs like "Louie Louie" and "Hang on Sloopy" utilize this classic group of changes, and once you play it, I'm sure you'll recognize the sound.

This kind of power chord grouping has shown up quite a bit in today's New Wave and pop music by singers such as Rick Springfield and Pat Benatar. It's also good practice for moving quickly from the open position to closed and for stretching the fingers. Listen to songs such as Springfield's "Jesse's Girl," and Benatar's "Hit Me With Your Best Shot" for this kind of chord change.

This power chord, though hardly used in an original sense today, along with the blues progression, probably made up three-quarters of the songs written from about 1956 to 1962! It's the progression most often associated with the "doo-wop" sound of the fifties, and though rarely used in hard rock, it's still a nice variation to have in your repertoire.

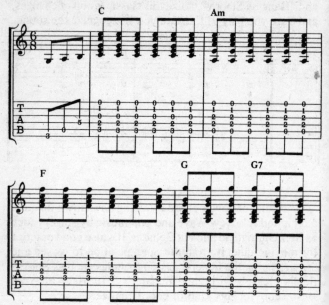

This very powerful chord change evokes the music of Jimi Hendrix, as well as such early blues greats as Muddy Waters and Howlin' Wolf. You can experiment with playing it in both the open and closed positions I've written out here for you.

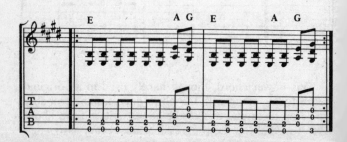

This minor key progression is reminiscent of some of rock's most haunting songs, such as Bob Dylan's "All Along the Watchtower," as played by Jimi Hendrix, "Stairway to Heaven," by Led Zeppelin, and others that featured powerful, extended guitar solos. You'll find that minor keys in general lend themselves to a more mournful, sad sound than do major keys, and this translates into a very expressive medium for the guitar. Try playing this exercise in several different tempos, feeling the various moods it can evoke.

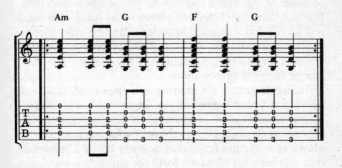

Chapter Five

LEARN ROCK LEAD GUITAR

Being a lead guitarist certainly has its responsibilities. More often than not, the lead player must assume the role of bandleader and, in many cases, is the songwriter and arranger of the music. Assuming you're not in this position but you're still the lead player in the band, you must still have a basic musical knowledge and be able to communicate this to the listener. This, of course can take many years to develop, though the training of your "ear" can be faster than you think.

In single-note-style playing it's important that you develop a "mind's eye" of the fingerboard. This fingerboard memorization is essential to developing improvisational skills, as we really think of what we are about to play a split second before we actually do. It's important that you take the ideas set forth for you in this book and go on and invent new personal approaches to your lead playing. In essence, that is what I hope to achieve with this book: the encouragement and inspiration to help you to go on to be a better player and to develop a style that is all your own.

The lead guitarist has many tools at his disposal and so is often the envy of players of other instruments, such as piano or drums. The guitar has such vocal capabilities, such as string-bending, vibrato, hammering-on and pulling-off, that it sometimes gives other instruments the appearance of being comparatively "static" in nature, with very little physical note-altering that can take place.

Some of these techniques can really present major learning obstacles for aspiring guitarists, and, in fact, these problems can remain unchanged for many, many years. I personally have had students come to me with as much as fifteen years' experience who still can't get the right vibrato or bend a string properly. When they do, however, it's a revelation, and it sure can pump new life into a tired style! Some students are lucky (making the teacher a lot happier, too), such as when I taught Ralph Macchio for *Crossroads*. He seemed to really possess the ability to intuitively recognize certain musical concepts just from being a fan of guitar music. He was therefore able to absorb such techniques as vibrato and string-bending more easily than many pupils I've had who'd already been playing for some time. This also must be due in part to the fact that he hadn't the chance to acquire any bad habits yet, while the more experienced players were *full* of problems that had to be dealt with. Just remember to avoid trying to go too hastily through the material, to take each hurdle one step at a time, and it'll be a lot more fun for you, and you'll be a much better player for it!

The Rock Scale Positions

In this scale, an extension of the initial open one we discussed earlier in the book, the last part of the scale is brought up higher on the fingerboard, allowing many more possibilities. Here are two basic forms of it. The latter is my hands-down choice for flexibility, while I feel the former to be a bit too static. These are both written out for the key of A.

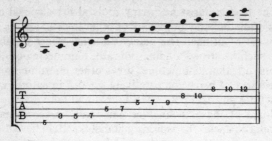

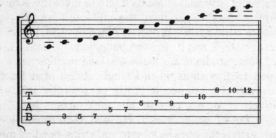

If we now add slides to the scale, enabling us to sometimes play two notes with only one pick of the string, we begin to see just how fluid this scale position can be.

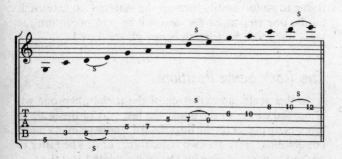

With the addition of some very well placed partial barres we can even further enhance the smoothness of this scale, as well as bring out more of its improvisational potential.

Make each one of these barres with the index finger, covering only two strings at a time.

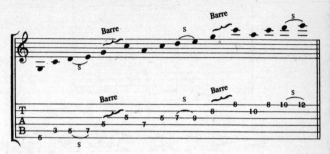

Hammer-on and Pull-off "Flash"

Getting back now to our earlier discussion of hammer-on and pull-off styles, we can now see how they apply to more advanced positions. Now, in these higher scale positions, the hammers and pulls become even more significant and can lend a great deal of flexibility and "flash" to your style.

Allowing the guitarist to play very fast successions of notes with this technique within a small area is one of its major benefits. We can now take scales and give them a lot more life and character, as well as much more speed. Here we see the two "closed" blues/rock positions, now utilizing this combination of pull-offs and hammer-ons. Note that we are still using some carefully placed slides between notes to help us change positions.

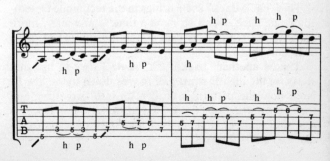

This "back-track" scale brings in the technique of actually going back over a string at a time to add many more notes to the pattern, as well as the illusion of yet more flash and speed.

This is another "back-track" scale I love to use that starts on the high E string and moves down to the low E. Note how the pattern is broken up into two-string and then three-string positions. Played rapidly, this lick is a real showstopper, and will be a good part of your vocabulary as a lead player.

Now, in our longest position, covering most of the neck, we see how the combination of hammers, pull-offs, *and* slides can make for some pretty interesting playing. It may take some time before you can coordinate all of these techniques into one smooth run, so please don't be discouraged; it took me years to develop it!

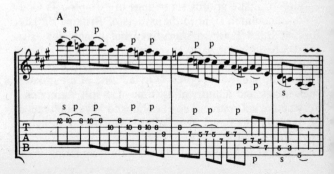

Eric Clapton *(Arlen Roth)*

Eric Clapton

It's hard to imagine any guitarist with more influence and achievements than Eric Clapton. Certainly the most important English guitarist to develop out of the classic blues influence, Clapton first gained recognition with The Yardbirds and John Mayall's Bluesbreakers, another band that gave birth to the careers of many a famous British rocker. His biggest impact was felt in the late sixties, however, with his power trio Cream. Their songs, such as "Sunshine of Your Love," "White Room," and "I'm So Glad," became rock anthems, and the guitar solos were enough to make graffiti scrawlings of "Clapton Is God" a not-uncommon sight in the streets of Britain. He later formed Blind Faith, a short-lived but nonetheless successful band in the early seventies. And with Derek and The Dominoes, a studio group that included the legendary Duane Allman, he recorded "Layla," one of the greatest rock songs and albums of all time. He still maintains a very active solo career and continues to have such recent hit records as "Lay Down Sally," "Wonderful Tonight," "Cocaine," and "Forever Man."

The first lick here is a classic—the two-string index

finger barre. It's reminiscent of the playing of stars such as Clapton and Jimmy Page. This barring should take the form of a sort of "curl" around the edge of the neck. You will get a cleaner tone on the high E string without feeling that you must press down extra-hard to achieve it.

This technique can be aided greatly by the use of partial barres, where two or three strings are covered at a time. These new positions are some of the most widely played when it comes to true "flash" playing, due to their relative convenience and flexibility. Try to play the high note with your third finger, stretching over the two-string index-finger barre.

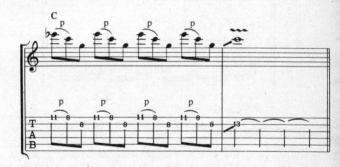

This ever-popular lick is basically the same as the previous one, only now you must make the pull-off on the B string. Be sure to arch your third finger enough so as not to accidentally damp out the tone of the high E string.

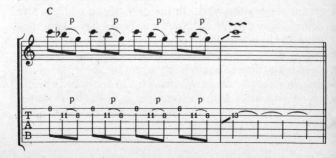

Doubling it up, or playing pull-offs on both top strings, can be a lot trickier than it initially seems. You must play this lick with an aggressive all-downstroke attack, trying to attain a fair amount of speed as you go along. Remember, don't try to play too fast too soon, or else you'll be stumbling over yourself needlessly. Just try to get these notes nice and even in both volume and sustain, and you'll be in good shape for this stage of the game!

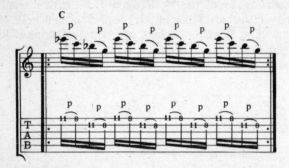

Passing Tones

There are many cases in both rock and blues guitar where the notes that apply 'go against the grain' of either the chord you are playing over or the scale. These *dissonant* tones are not part of the scale and chord and are sometimes referred to as "passing" notes. I like to call them that because they are, more often than not, the notes we've been passing over while making whole-step jumps in our single-note work. In the case of the scales we've been working with so far, these notes have lain right beneath the *slides* we've been playing. They are the *flatted fifths* of the scale, and have a decidedly dissonant sound. You don't need to worry about the theory involved, just concentrate on how it *sounds*. To see what I mean, try playing an A Major chord with an E flat in it. Rather strange, isn't it? In any event, these are the "blue" notes you hear musicians refer to so often, and they are the central focus of countless licks and solos in rock music. Here is your first open-position rock scale, with the addition now of these flatted-fifth "blue" notes.

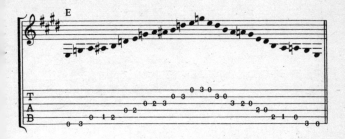

If we now take it up to the closed position, we see where the flatted fifths now lie. Try playing them in two ways. Play them first using the third finger after the second has played the note below it, then as a continuous slide that is played by the same finger. The latter way of playing the scale will accentuate its feeling of movement from one position to another and will more closely resemble the way we played the scale without the flatted fifths.

The longer scale position uses the "flat-fives" very effectively as well and is the source for some of the hottest rock licks around!

This group of pull-off licks will be instantly recognizable to you. They all utilize the flatted fifth for that really bluesy sound, and in each case they should be played with the index, middle, and ring fingers. The open position pull-off licks, of course, don't need the index finger—due to the use of open strings—however, you might find the open-position pull-offs easier to execute with the index and middle as opposed to the middle and ring fingers. Give each way a try and see what is most comfortable for your hands.

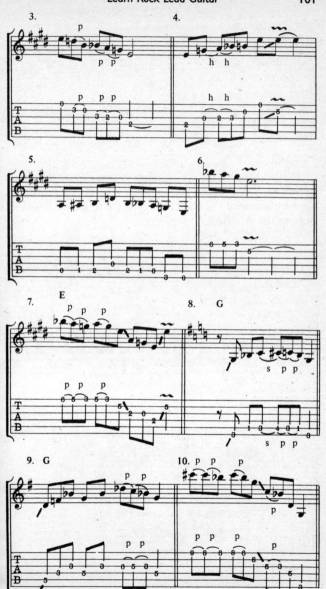

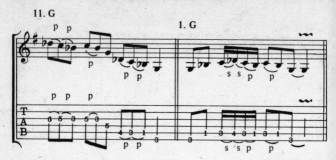

Substituting *slides* for the first two notes of this type of pull-off lick can help your speed a lot and is particularly appropriate with the use of the lower strings, such as the lick on the A string.

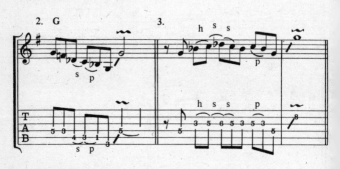

A quick slide up and down can create some pretty fantastic-sounding runs. It will take some time before these become accurate, because one usually tends to overshoot the frets when first attempting licks such as these. Play all the up-down slides with the third finger, and then make the pull-off to the note a whole step below.

String-Bending

The ability to bend strings is probably the single most enviable thing a guitarist can do. It certainly is the most "vocal" of all guitar techniques and enables the guitarist to become extremely expressive with his or her instrument. The very act of bending a string takes a certain degree of emotional commitment, which is quite evident in the sound of the great string benders. I have always loved this technique, and it finds its way into almost anything or any style I play.

There are many great players who have made string-bending an integral part of their sound, even though their methods have varied greatly over the years. There are blues players who have always bent with a lot of vibrato, such as Eric Clapton and Mike Bloomfield and Otis Rush, while there are blues artists, such as B. B. King and Buddy Guy, who use less vibrato on their bends while relying heavily upon vibrato for their single-note work.

Although the styles of string-bending do vary greatly, there are some very important rules to follow if you expect to make this a viable part of your guitar-playing. The first and perhaps most important rule is always to use as many fingers as are available *behind* the bending finger to help the bend along. This is, of course, provided that the bend involves only one note and that no other notes are being held down. It is essential that the entire hand be committed to the bending process, with the thumb curling over the edge of the fingerboard. This helps to apply opposite "squeezing" pressure when bending *toward* you, while it also serves as an anchor for pivoting when you are bending *away* from you. With the exception of the high E string, all index-finger-only bends should take the form of a *pivot* away from you. This pivoting point is on the side of the index finger, just below the large knuckle, and it rests on the side of the neck. The basic principle behind the pivot is that you don't really concern yourself with the tip of your finger; rather, you should make the pivot and let the bend occur as a result of the pivoting motion itself. This will give your hand a kind of "set" position for bending in this manner and will help in accuracy and consistency. Refer to the photos for proper position.

When bending with either the second or third finger, use the other fingers to bend it along as well. In fact, upon closer examination over the years, I've noticed that my index finger not only bends but helps to push the other strings out of the way *for* the bent string when it bends toward me. Therefore, when the bend is released and the string is returned to its original position, the index finger

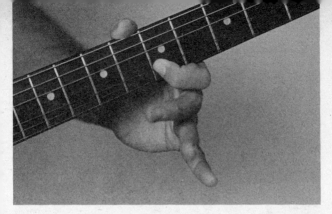

Position for index finger bend. Note how it "pivots" from the side of the neck *(Deborah Roth)*

then lingers awhile over the lower strings, damping out any unwanted noises or notes that may occur. This may sound rather simple, but I have had students come to me with fifteen years of playing experience who still don't understand how to get a clean bent note! When you're bending down and *away* from you, you should still use all the fingers that are available to help the bend, while the thumb curls over the lower strings as a damping action. Please refer to the photos for these positions as well.

A three-fingered bend toward you *(Deborah Roth)*

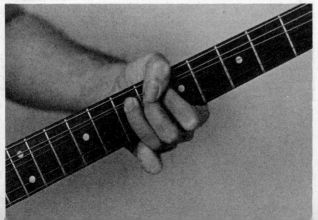

A three-fingered bend away from you *(Deborah Roth)*

The following group of scales is written out here with circles around the notes I would recommend bending. Try to bend them with the pitch of the next note in mind and see how well you do. This should only be a preliminary bending exercise for you, as string-bending is a rather painful and strenuous technique for the newcomer and should be approached carefully.

Here are some bending licks just to get you used to the technique and to how far you should bend the strings. It will become very important that you develop a feeling of just how far strings should be bent in advance, as there will be many times when you must bend a note up "silently" even before it is sounded, which requires true accuracy. The first group of bends are *toward* you, while the second are *away*.

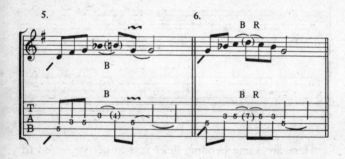

There are many times when either a bend will be played in combination with another fretted note or that other note will be played very soon after the bend has occurred. This usually takes place when there is a third-finger bend, with the fretted note played on a higher adjacent string. Here is a case where you must bend toward you, while your pinky stays on the same fret on the next string. This will require some discipline to master, because the anchored finger will always try to "follow" the bending fingers. After a while, however, the independence will develop.

Here is the same position, only now the notes are phrased separately, with the bend up to pitch occurring twice. This is a very important stylistic approach to rock guitar.

Frequently a note is bent up to a pitch and then the same pitch is played in its unbent form on the next string. This is also a crucial style in rock and blues guitar, and it represents one of the earlier forms of blues and rock phrasing. The real trick within this position is what I call the ability to "get in and get out" during the bending process. In other words, the bend is created with the use of three fingers, including the index. Then, while the bend is held up, the index finger must quickly abandon the role of bend-helper to play the note that lies on the high E string. This creates a momentary weakness in the bend and will result in some flattening of pitch for the unexperienced player. After a while, however, the two remaining bending fingers will learn to compensate for the slight loss of power, and they'll be able to maintain the bend's original pitch without a falter.

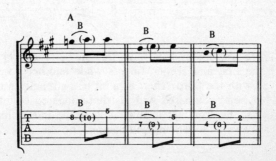

This kind of position is often followed with a phrase that involves a release of the bend, a pull-off, and then a rebending of the same note. The release-and-pull-off process is an interesting one, for the release occurs in one direction, while the pull-off's "pluck" is in another. You'll see that the more you play this, the more it will make sense to you physically.

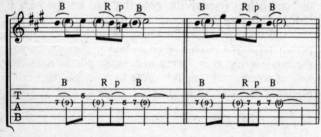

There are some special bends that are better off played with the first and second fingers while another note is played with the third. There is a bit less strength in this kind of bend compared with its three-fingered counterpart, but the fact that it still involves the index finger gives it adequate bending and damping power.

Special Rock Licks

This is a collection of some of the most important and "hottest" licks to have under your belt at this time. I've deliberately jumped back and forth between the open and closed positions, and, of course, I've included many bends. Remember that you will derive the most from these exercises if you proceed slowly. You really stand to get frustrated if you attempt to be a master overnight; even the biggest rock star spent countless hours practicing these licks. Anyway, I hope you enjoy learning and playing these licks, and I hope they become a permanent part of your guitar vocabulary, as well as allow you to come up with some new ideas of your own.

Vibrato

No discussion of rock guitar techniques and styles would be complete without some mention of vibrato. This is the wavering, vibrating sound that is created by the fretting finger making the note sustain much longer than usual and giving it a decidedly "vocal" quality. Also one of the guitarist's main expressive tools, each person's vibrato is like his own fingerprint. Well-known vibrato techniques that come to mind are those of B. B. King, Otis Rush, Eric Clapton, Mike Bloomfield, and each of these players represents certain distinctive approaches to vibrato playing. It should be pointed out here that this is mainly an acoustic nylon-string approach and deals primarily with the sound of string against wood. While rock guitar vibrato is not the same as the classical style of vibrato, where the wavering is created expressly by the hand moving up and down, much like a violinist's, it is similar. The classical-style vibrato really isn't appropriate to electric guitar, and anyway, it takes too much effort to get *any* vibrato with it. This style was popular with the West Coast acid rock musicians in the late sixties but isn't used much these days.

Straight vibrato, where you do not bend the string, is created primarily by a rapid *pivoting* motion of the left hand, unlike the violinist's rapid *up-and-down* motion. This pivot comes from the side of the index finger that is below the large knuckle and is against the side of the neck. It's important that the vibrato hand be as free from the neck as possible, so that the *only* points touching the neck are the tip of the finger and the pivoting point. Therefore, the vibrato effect is caused by the hand's pivot, in which the turning of the fingertip makes the string waver. This anchored pivoting point makes it very difficult to accidentally bend too far and will enable you to control the vibrato to be as slow or fast as you want. Perhaps the finest and best-known purveyor of this type of vibrato is B. B. King. So much so that I refer to this hand position as the "B. B. King butterfly," because of the butterflylike motion the hand goes through when making this rapid pivot.

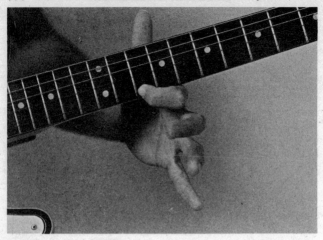

Position for the index finger bend. Note how it "pivots" from the side of the neck *(Deborah Roth)*

Ready to "pivot" to create vibrato

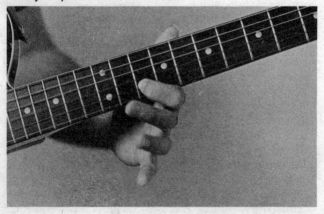

If you wish to create the vibrato with either the second, third, or fourth finger, the index finger should be on the string, below the top fingers, as you are still using the pivot for the vibrato action. You'll note that this technique is very similar to what we must do in proper string-bending. I should also mention that when using the pivot vibrato style, the motion is always down-return, down-return. In other words, you never push up, toward you, and the first action is always down, *away* from you.

VIBRATO AND STRING-BENDING

Combining vibrato with the technique of string-bending is an entirely different matter and is an extremely tough technique to master properly. Obviously, we can bend *away* from us and still use the pivoting point from which to make the vibrato, but whether we bend away from *or* toward us, the vibrato directly depends on a bend-and-release action that is hard to maintain. Without question, the first problem you'll encounter with this technique is maintaining the pitch as you begin the vibrato. Even on records, I hear well-known players unable to hold up the bend and give it vibrato, which makes for some rather sour notes! When bending a note toward you, you must visualize it as a slight bend-release action creating the vibrato. The times when we must bend toward us instead of away are usually when the notes that follow the bend are on strings that are above the bent string. In this manner, we can go from the bend to the fretted notes relatively smoothly and with a minimum of extraneous sound. See the photos for the proper positions.

When I teach this vibrato style to my students, I emphasize the fact that the bend must first be up to pitch, with the vibrato action started soon after. This can be likened to a singer's vibrato that seems to start after the note has been sung for a while.

Here are some licks to get you started with this style. Again, try to bend the note up to pitch first, and then, while it's sustaining, begin the slight, even give-and-take action required to create the vibrato. Remember, this is a very different way of playing the vibrato technique, and it requires great finger control and independence. Once you master it though, you'll have a lot of players knocking at your door, asking you how it's done!

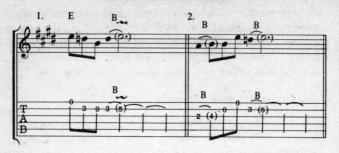

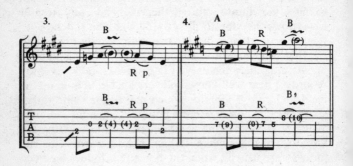

When we start to combine straight bends with vibrato bends in the same lick, we are really controlling our instruments and making them "speak." This is another case of "getting in and getting out," particularly when the bends occur within a short span of time of one another and involve different strings. This group of runs illustrates this style.

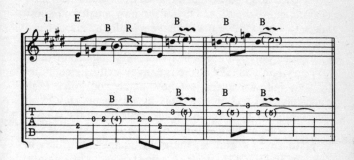

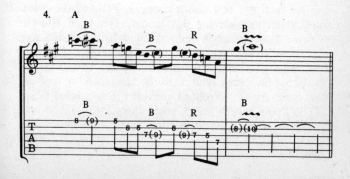

Beginning Rock Soloing

When you can take a full-fledged solo or lead break in a song or a jamming situation, you're unleashing all your experience and knowledge into a very concentrated period of time and expression. Obviously, how much you know and how long you've played have a profound effect upon your solos, and I find that I can usually "hear the years" in a given guitarist's playing. One very important thing you do when you take a solo is convey to the listener and to your fellow players just how much you know both musically and technically. This by no means should be interpreted as a license to always "pull out all the stops," but rather as a chance to mold a solo into just what *you* want to say. Of course, there are many intangibles in soloing, and in music itself. A solo stands out in a unique way within the song or musical piece and has a structure which is a statement made by the soloist. This statement is determined solely by you, the player; the structure you choose embodies your statement.

So far we've been discussing licks that basically stand on their own and apply to one chord. One of the special aspects of soloing is that most of the time you must solo over more than one chord. This chord "change" is something that must be conveyed and expressed in your soloing and often means only a very subtle change in order to work.

Within the scales we already know, there are certain notes, which seem to lie right beneath our fingers, that can be used for new chord changes. Perhaps the most applicable situation for this is the often-used I-to-IV change. This change is very commonplace in rock, and you needn't stray very far from the I chord's position to find some good notes for improvisation. This diagram illustrates the blues scale with the applicable as well as new notes for the IV chord encircled. I've cricled them so you know *exactly* which notes apply to the IV chord. Note how close to the old position some of the new notes are.

Here is a simple I-IV change that illustrates what I've been talking about. Note the subtle changes that are taking place, and try to train your ear to recognize the new IV chord within the notes you're playing. This is a really essential part of learning to improvise properly: hearing what you want to play just before you actually play it.

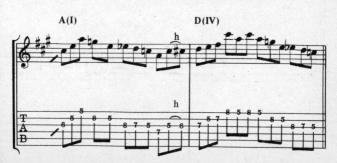

This I-IV improvisation utilizes *chromatic*-style notes to achieve some of the new changes. This is a style primarily based upon the usage of notes that follow each other fret by fret, half-step by half-step. In chromatic-style playing there is rarely any space left between notes. This lends itself to a very fast and fluid way of picking, and the hand can carry itself through a very large number of notes in a very short time. It is a good tool for the lead player, because the chromatic style enables him or her to "walk" to the new changes, creating a true feeling of movement, as well as a sense of the new chord change "approaching."

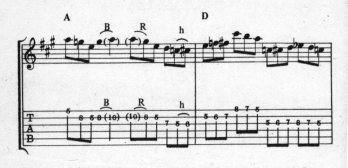

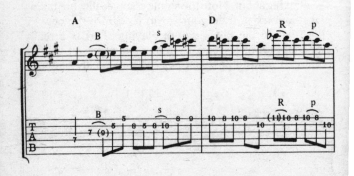

The use of a *seventh* within one chord can also serve to *anticipate* the new change, and this is, of course, also evident in rhythm guitar playing. You'll notice that in this exercise we are using the seventh within the scale *just* before we make the shift to the IV chord. See if you can recognize this particular style in other music you've heard. Please note that you can always find the seventh of a particular chord by finding the note that exists one whole step—two frets—below the root. Hence, the seventh of E would be D, A would be G, and so on.

The V, or dominant, chord is also a very often-used change from either the I or the IV and, again, the V shares many common notes with the I as well as notes that are very close to the original rock scale positions. This chart shows just where many of these notes lie; both the new notes and the old scale notes that apply to the V are encircled.

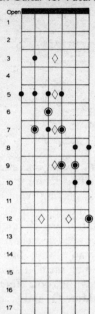

This is a simple and rather quick I-IV-V change to help illustrate just where many of these notes lie and how accessible they are to you. The major sevenths, lying one fret below the root, become particularly useful when expressing the V chord, and you should learn to recognize their sound, as well as their positions on the neck.

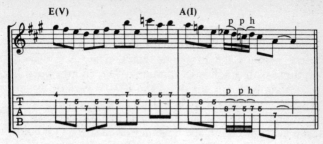

Now we reverse two chords and make it a I-V-IV progression. The positions are not changed very much, but the general approach is, because the musical statement is so different.

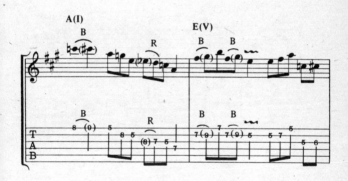

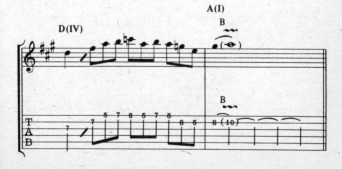

SOLOS

The following will be a big step for you. These are full-length lead rock solos around various changes and represent perhaps the first time you'll have ever played anything with a soloistic approach. The chords we will be dealing with are mostly of the I-IV-V variety, as the preceding exercises were based upon this musical pattern. Note how we sometimes use bends that are common to more than one chord, and how they often sustain for quite some time. This will take a fair amount of strength on your part, as you'll have to maintain the pitch of the bend for more than one beat. The first solo deals with a I-IV-V progression.

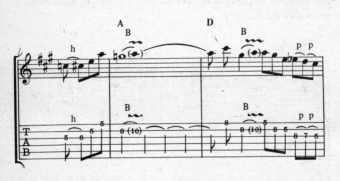

This piece emphasizes the special soloing style that occurs between the I chord and its relative minor, or VI minor. If we move the blues/rock scale A down a step and a half, or three frets, we now have the *major pentatonic* scale for the same chord. If we juxtapose this same scale against the relative minor of *that chord*, it now takes on the characteristics of being the *blues* scale for the new chord! The relative minor of A is F#M and has the same characteristics as the blues scale for the A chord.

I know this sounds like an awful lot of theory to swallow right now, but all we are really saying is that one scale, the major pentatonic, has a decidedly "up" and "optimistic" sound to it, while the blues scale has a more somber, sad tone. They, however are really the *same* scale, only juxtaposed against two *different* chords, giving them a complete change of character. This is one of the lead guitar's most pleasant phenomena, and it has been put to good use over the decades in countless classic rock songs. Obviously, we don't want to merely think that we can play the same notes over two chord changes as our easy way out, for though these chords share a common scale, we are drastically altering the sound of these notes by juxtaposing them against new chords. Therefore, we must accentuate different notes over each respective chord, putting our emotional emphasis in different areas each time. You'll see what I mean in the following solo, particularly in the case of the bent notes.

There are many times when a certain "tension" is maintained as a scale is insistently worked over with varying chord changes. This is quite apparent in a lot of the great rock solos and is a great source of emotional and musical ideas. One of the more common situations in which this "tension" occurs is the I-VII change. In this kind of progression we, for example, would stick completely to our blues/rock notes for both the E chord and the D, even though the D chord is trying to attract us to itself! The I-VII-IV classic rock progression is perfect for showing this particular theory, and the IV chord acts as a nice semi-resolved chord to work with as a release of the D chord's tension. "Resolution" means that we go through the different chord changes and end up on a consonant chord—one that is not dissonant from the root. In this case, the IV chord implies the sound of the root chord without it actually being played.

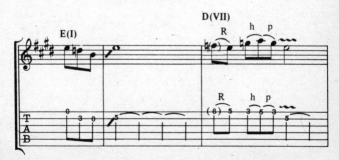

Chapter Six

HEAVY METAL GUITAR

Over the past few years, heavy-metal music has enjoyed one of music's great comebacks. At the core of this hard-hitting sound is some of the most dynamic and inventive guitar work around. The roots of this style are once again based upon the blues; however, classical composers, such as Bach and Paganini, are having an increasingly profound effect upon some of metal's young guitar greats. While some of metal's forefathers, such as Jimi Hendrix and Jimmy Page, were mainly blues-influenced, we see new guitar greats, such as Steve Vai and Yngwie Malmsteen, taking from the scales of the great classical composers, as well as other non-American influences, such as Indian and Middle Eastern music. This new scale sense has been steadily moving into rock's mainstream, and guitarists and synthesists everywhere are changing their sound. Of course, heavy metal and *all* lead guitar styles owe themselves to the blues and early rock 'n' roll, no matter how far away it may stray from the roots. It is very important that you keep this in mind, because if you don't, your playing will be lacking quite a lot, and who wants to only sound like today's model, soon to become obsolete?

The development of the guitar has really been like a family tree. You can start with, for example, a great acoustic delta bluesman, such as Bukka White or Robert Johnson, then have a B. B. King listening to him and becoming inspired to take the music somewhere else, then Eric Clapton, far away in England, emulating B.B.'s style and coming up with one all his own, then Eddie Van Halen growing up loving Clapton and ending up a star. Needless to say, there are plenty of future stars listening to today's musicians, and we'll look forward to what they have to offer in the years to come.

One of the current heavy-metal strong points is the blazing speed at which some of these solos and licks are played. Players like Randy Rhoads, Van Halen, Steve Vai, and Brad Gillis have all taken the guitar's speed to new heights, and while speed isn't everything, it's something the rock guitarist should have in his arsenal. Personally, I prefer to hold the speed-work in reserve and play these flurries of notes when I feel they are needed, rather than constantly playing at top speed.

Getting Faster: Chromatic and "Stretch" Exercises

In heavy-metal, the additional speed usually comes from the picking hand, as opposed to the fretting hand. This will require a great deal of practice and hard work, and for some it can almost be too much! I know this from personal experience, as I became very content and almost complacent with my ability to play rapidly with the aid of left-hand acrobatics such as hammer-ons and pull-offs. There is nothing wrong with being "left-hand fast," but it is only part of the story. Playing in a chromatic style and making up new chromatic runs yourself is one of the quickest ways of developing an attack that is well balanced between both hands. It's important to remember that the right hand should be *over* the strings, attacking each string at just about the same angle. This is crucial to developing good picking speed, as it enables you to "float" over the strings while you keep the wrist and forearm as relaxed as possible.

Keeping the wrist relaxed as you move across the strings

This is a basic chromatic run that will help you develop your picking speed. The notes are in groups of three, played by the first, second, and third fingers respectively. Be sure to keep them moving up, one note at a time, in perfect synch, with the right hand picking. Pick down-up-down, up-down-up, etc.

Now we can experiment with the four-fingered chromatic style, walking the notes up in groups of four. This is a good exercise for getting the pinky in shape, and it is an area in which many rock guitarists are deficient. The angle at which you arch the fingers over the fretboard is crucial here, and we now move away from the usual left-hand rock position to the more poised jazz or classical position.

Proper position for the chromatic jazz style

Chromatic runs can be really helpful in playing a fast, heavy-metal style of lead guitar, and they can be created all over the fretboard. In this exercise, we take what is basically our long blues/rock scale and substitute chromatic runs where fret jumps would normally occur. You'll find this particularly entertaining, due to its tricky nature, and I recommend that you use your first three fingers for the chromatic run-up licks.

Here are some very useful chromatic licks that you can add to your repertoire. Note how in some of them the chromatic lick is continued over to other adjacent strings. These will require particularly deft right-hand picking, so keep that wrist relaxed!

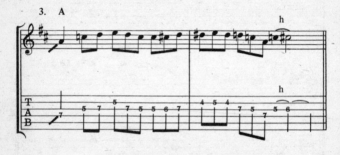

Here are some excellent four-fingered stretches to help your hand become more acquainted with this position in heavy-metal playing. This again requires rapid picking, and remember to keep the angle of the pick as consistent as possible from string to string. (See photo for left-hand position.)

"Stretching" the left hand

This pentatonic-scale run uses similar stretches to achieve a more melodic approach than the previous exercise. The starting note should be played with the second finger, while the main stretches should occur between the index and pinky.

This diminished-scale run is always handy to have in the repertoire, not to mention its being another great left-hand stretch exercise. Experiment playing it with the first and third fingers in the rock position, and also with the first and fourth fingers for the jazz/classical position.

Van Halen–Style Two-Handed Hammer-ons

Perhaps no guitarist since the early days of Eric Clapton has had as much of an impact on music as Edward Van Halen. He is truly a revolutionary stylist, and his two-handed hammer-on technique has spawned a new generation of rock guitarists, all of whom now include this technique in their vocabulary. Besides playing on all the hits of his own band, Van Halen, he also played the solo on Michael Jackson's "Beat It," a lead break of monumental proportions. This crossover from heavy metal to the mainstream of rock and pop is indicative of metal's newfound acceptance and much of the credit must go to Eddie Van Halen and the Van Halen sound.

No style is so closely associated with heavy-metal lead guitar as Eddie Van Halen's two-handed fingerboard hammer-ons. This technique is a great "flash" style, as well as an effective way to stretch the guitarist's fingerboard abilities beyond the scope of what is usually possible. Vastly overused and overexposed these days, it certainly doesn't make or break a heavy-metal player, but

Eddie Van Halen *(Glen La Ferman)*

it's a good technique to experiment with and to have under your belt.

There are basically two types of right-hand hammer-ons that can be used. The first and most common one is when the right hand hammers-on to a note *above*—in terms of pitch—the highest note the left hand has played; the second is when the right hand comes over and frets a note that is *below*—again, lower in pitch—what the left hand will now be hammering onto. The latter is a bit trickier but can offer some astounding possibilities.

Position for right-hand hammer-ons, or "tapping"

Position for two-handed hammer-pull.

Before you try playing more melodic passages with this technique, I think it's important that you get a basic feel for how it should be played. Perhaps the most often-used approach for this style is the quick hammer-pull. This happens when the left hand already has a pattern that is fretted, while the right hand hammers-on one note and then pulls off to the lower left-hand notes. This can be used as a very showy, flashy technique and, with some practice, can be played at lightning speed. The pull-off occurs much in the way you've learned so far; after the hammer-on by your index finger has occurred, you simply pull-off, down and *away* from you, while the left hand holds down the other notes securely. Then, of course, the next hammer-on is created in the traditional left-hand manner. Here is your first two-hand pattern, for the high E string.

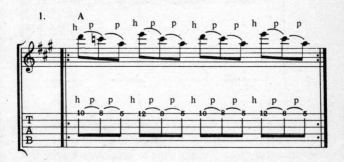

Here is a complete pattern, covering all the strings, that utilizes the same two-handed position. You'll probably notice that it starts to get a little crowded when you move onto the middle strings and that extreme accuracy is required to make the right-hand hammer-pull cleanly. This is why I don't recommend trying this onstage in a too dimly lit club!

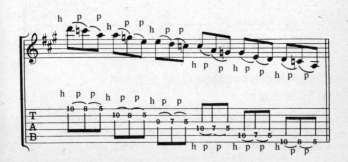

In this pattern, we see another "flash" technique emerge. While we are maintaining the right-hand and index-finger positions, the middle note is alternating between two frets. This now affords us the ability to make it sound quite a bit more melodic and is a bit more of an "illusionary"-sounding lick.

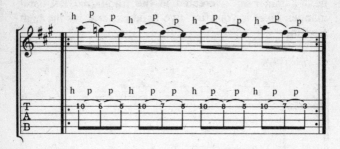

Of course, if we change the position of the right-hand hammer-on, we can really stretch out and play some positions that truly sound impossible to be played by the left hand alone!

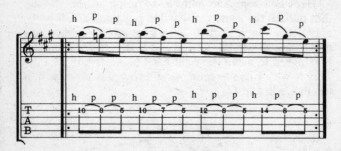

COMBINING RIGHT-HAND HAMMER-ONS WITH BENDS

One of my favorite approaches for this heavy-metal technique is to combine it with notes that are bent. It's particularly interesting because the bend now affects the right-hand hammer-on as much as anything else, adding more melodic possibilities to your playing. For example, in this little exercise the bend on the seventh fret of the G string now makes the hammer-on to the twelfth sound like the fourteenth. This has a distinctive "yodeling" sound to it, particularly since it goes from the fifth of the chord up to a higher octave of the root. Once the high note is sounded, help it sustain by use of left-hand vibrato. The effect will really be exciting!

If you create a bend-and-release situation in tandem with a right-hand hammer-on, you will really start to see just how much the notes can be controlled. Here we bend, hammer-on, then release the bend, and finally pull-off.

Now we will reverse the situation and use the right hand as the "foundation" on which all of the left-hand's

activities occur. This is necessary mainly because the left
hand has stronger and more accurate hammer-on and pull-
off powers than the right hand. Still, we can play in this
way and then, in a real "flash" move, bring the right hand
back over to play some high hammer-ons as well!

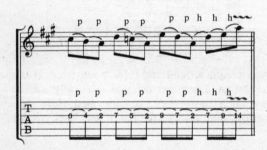

If we start to use all four fingers of the left hand in
addition to the right-hand hammer-ons, we are playing
some pretty advanced stuff! It may take you a while to
get the pinky to hammer-on strongly enough to make the
note sustain properly. It would be beneficial to play this
at a fairly loud volume, as it will help smooth out the
notes and create a great deal more helpful sustain to work
with. Anyway, how much quiet heavy metal have you
heard lately?

Other "Flash" Techniques

The right-hand hammer-on approach is a relatively new phenomenon in guitar playing, and there have been countless flashy players who never even attempted this style! Players such as Jimmy Page, Jimi Hendrix, and others who helped forge the heavy-metal style resorted to more traditional means of getting the most out of their instruments. Of course, Jimi Hendrix was using stacks of amps and developed feedback control into a fine art, while Jimmy Page was playing with a violin bow and Pete Townshend was smashing his guitars, so I wouldn't call all of their techniques traditional! What I'm really referring to is the traditional two hands in the usual place! Jimi Hendrix used the vibrato bar to a great extent, and, in fact, this has also become a major part of today's heavy-metal technique. (See earlier chapter on equipment for vibrato bar details.) Had it not been for his experiments with feedback and vibrato bar "roars" and "screams," you probably would not hear as much of it today. Jimi was a master at being able to pick while holding the bar in the same hand. This is really the only way you can get a smooth attack with the bar, and it enables you to use it in many subtle ways.

Position for holding the vibrato bar while using the flatpick

I like to play a run with the vibrato bar in my picking hand and then single out certain notes to be affected by the tremolo action of the bar. For this approach, I hold the bar against the palm of my hand, while the pick is gripped between the thumb and forefinger, just after the end of the bar. As I play across the strings, the bar swings with my wrist, ready to be used at any time. Here is a run that picks out just a few notes to be played with the vibrato bar. Try playing them with a fast vibrato, and then with a slow, even vibrato.

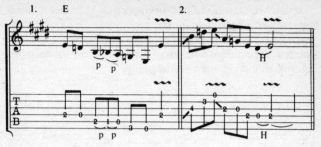

One use of the vibrato bar that is particularly attractive involves allowing the note to be "silently" dropped with the bar, and then picked and returned to its normal pitch. This works equally well with harmonics and fretted notes. Try playing this run smoothly and slowly, and make the silent "dips" about a whole step down in pitch, as indicated in the music and tablature.

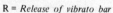

R = *Release of vibrato bar*

Here are a group of pull-off licks that stylistically lend themselves to the vibrato bar technique. In some of the ones that involve constant repetitive pull-offs, you might want to experiment with long, drawn-out dips, where the pitch keeps dropping and dropping.

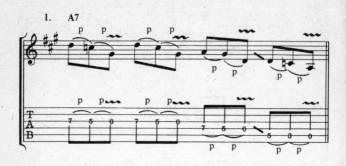

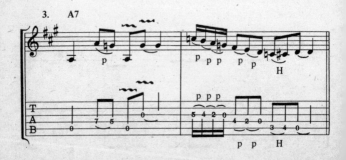

LEFT-HAND BARRES FOR FLASH

Partial barres played by the left hand are probably more responsible for lead guitar "flash" than any other single technique. This is because they enable you to create a foundation from which to make many very rapid hammer-ons and pull-offs without a great deal of effort. Of course, earlier in the book we discussed some of the more basic applications of these partial barres, but here we will spice them up with the addition of bends.

In this position, we bend up a whole step on the G string, then barre over the top two strings. The note we are bending to on the G is the same as the next note we play on the adjacent B string. Make sure to play this note just as the G string bend reaches the right pitch. This is a great ear-training device and will eventually help your bending accuracy a great deal.

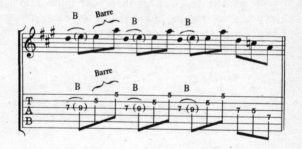

Now we play the same lick, only we finish it off with a really nice bend up to the root. Since this bend occurs at the end of the lick, you can again have the luxury of using the entire hand for it. This will enable you to sustain it longer and thereby help the vibrato process.

One of my all-time favorite "flash" licks combines the bends with the partial barre in a very exciting, rapid-fire display of guitar fireworks! You can hear this type of playing in the attack of just about every heavy-metal guitarist; it has been a mainstay of lead guitar since the days of Eric Clapton and Cream.

In this particular lick, we are relying upon the barre's sustaining capabilities for hammer-ons and pull-offs. They do go by quickly, but if the barre is not solid enough, the notes will come out fuzzy. Once the lick is in full gear, you might find it more advantageous to bend the G string with your second finger rather than your third. Practice it slowly at first, making sure that all the elements and pitches are happening properly, then you can experiment with speeding it up. Good luck with it!

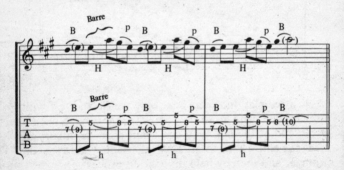

Chapter Seven

ROCK SOLOS

This is the section I've been preparing you for all along. It's now your chance to show what you can do while you develop your timing and your ear to an even greater extent. Soloing should, of course, really be your own material, the notes your own creation. However, in the case of the exercises that follow, I'll be showing you some of my ideas on soloing over some of rock's most classic progressions. Hopefully, they will allow you to come up with some of your own new ideas and help you to develop your soloistic vocabulary. After all, these chord sequences will invariably turn up again in your guitar travels, so it will be helpful for you to have a better understanding of how to treat particular circumstances.

When you practice these solos, it might be a good idea for you to have another guitarist, bassist, or keyboard player play the changes behind you. If this isn't possible, I'd recommend that you record the chords on a tape player of some sort and then do your *own* lead playing to it! This is a lot of fun and will help your timing and accuracy during practice. It's really crucial that you come to a better understanding of what is being said musically by the solos, and the only way this can occur is by your getting used to hearing the chord changes you must play "against."

The first solo utilizes the classic I-IV-V blues progression. Listen to the subtle pitch changes in the bends as well as how the notes relate to the chords. Blues can be very melodic, too, and this solo will certainly bear out that point to you.

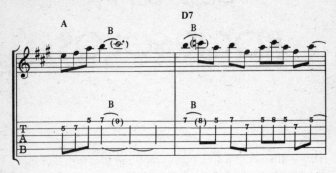

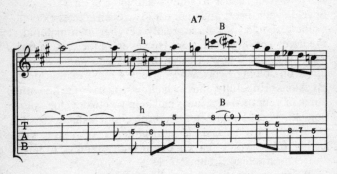

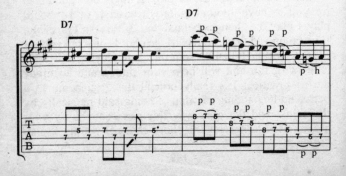

Changing these chords around doesn't really alter the positions as much as it does their *treatment*. This is really songwriting in its purest and simplest state, for by merely rearranging a group of chords, we can create an entirely new mood, both musically and emotionally.

This I-VII-IV progression is among the "heaviest" of the heavy-metal chord sequences. It also really brings out a lot of the tension of this form of lead guitar and has provided us with some of rock's best screaming solos. Note how though we're staying mostly in the same general area on the fretboard, the new chords create some rather powerful musical changes for both the player and the listener. Be sure to get all of the bends right!

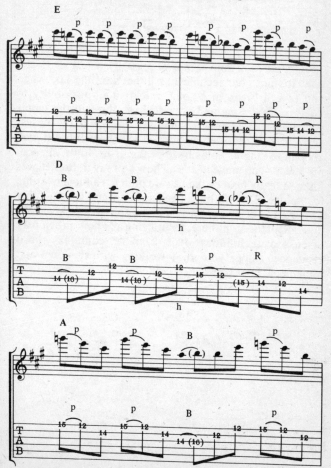

A good rock solo is not necessarily a fast or flashy one. It's not your technical skill that's on the line when you take a break in a song; rather, it's your ability to interpret that song and your feelings through the guitar in a given span of time. I would say that one of the easiest ways to know a true classic solo is to remember it well enough to sing it. Solos have peaks, rises, lows, silence, screams—you name it. It's all how you say it. Sometimes I like to really hold back in a solo until it's almost overdue to explode. This shifting of gears, as it were, is something I've tried to bring out for you in the solo that follows. We pull out all the stops here, by utilizing all of our previously discussed techniques over a more complex chord sequence. I hope you enjoy working with this one, and remember: hold back, *then* explode!

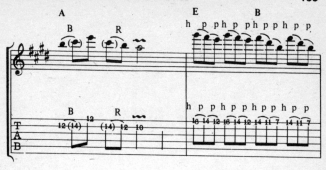

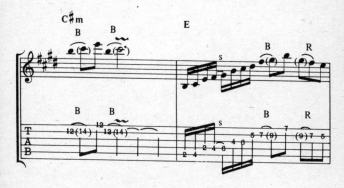

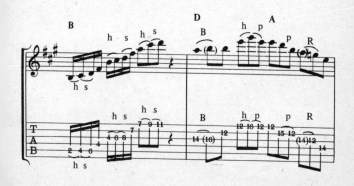

Chapter Eight

FORMING A BAND

Okay, you've got some playing under your belt; now you want to put it to real use. I can well remember the frustration of knowing at a very young age just how good I really was, yet not having anyone to play with or for. Believe me, the best audience you can have is your peers, and if there are very few around, or if the ones you do play with don't really listen, it can be a very frustrating time.

I grew up in the Bronx, in an area where there were six-story apartment buildings for as far as the eye could see. It was a great neighborhood, but a rough place to find musicians and an even harder place to rehearse! I still hold the theory that the majority of bands and musicians who made it big came from rural or suburban areas, where they lived in houses that had places to rehearse, such as garages and basements. What came out of my region? The classic *a capella* "doo-wop" streetcorner singing. A style consisting solely of vocals, without any instrumental accompaniment. All you needed for this was a corner or a well-reverberating high school bathroom and you had it made. It also wasn't very loud, and it couldn't have disturbed the neighbors the way my guitar playing did! Well, when I did form my first group, in 1965, at the ripe old age of twelve, I had to find someone with either a house (some did exist in the Bronx!) or an apartment that was surrounded by well-pacified neighbors. I guess it made sense that it was the drummer's apartment that we would rehearse in, for he was certainly the loudest, and *had* to be either loved or hated by the folks in the apartments around him.

As it turned out, my little band became quite popular, especially where we got our initial start, at my junior high school. The school was sometimes a place of rehearsal for us, as many of our shows were right there, and we proved to not be such a bad bunch of rock 'n' roll kids after all!

School is probably the first place you'll discover people to play with, and your seeing them frequently will help in the discovery of your musical likes and dislikes. Of course, it may not be all that easy for you to find the musicians you'd like to play with, but if you put out the call, someone will respond. You can put ads up on bulletin boards in your school or place an ad in one of the local papers. In fact, many papers are full of this kind of ad already, and you may find just who you're looking for in one issue. This is also, I might add, a great way to come across used equipment.

All right, so suppose you've found the right people, or are at least on your way. Now it's really time to get down to rehearsing and to playing some live "gigs." I know that there were times when I was guilty of "overrehearsing" while not playing live often enough. This is something to keep in mind, because you really don't know what you've got as a guitarist or as a band until you play in front of people. Playing live puts me on a higher "plane" musically, and I find myself listening to live tapes to relearn some licks I created on the spot in front of the crowd. This higher need to communicate is a crucial part of being a musician, and it can really be satisfied only in live performance situations. When you do rehearse, try to keep this in mind, and be sure to let *all* members of the band have a say in decisions about the music. It's very important that a healthy balance of musical responsibility be maintained within a group, as each member must feel that he or she is contributing. I do, however, feel that there should always be a "leader" in a band situation, one who makes the final decision and to whom the others look for encouragement, support, and ideas. This person is more often than not the lead guitarist, as he or she is apt to be the band's writer or arranger. Certainly, if the song you are working on is your own original composition, the others will *expect* a certain degree of leadership on your part when working out the band's arrangement. This leadership can take many forms, depending upon the kinds of musicians you're working with.

Over the years, I've become fondest of working with other players I can "trust." This means that in general I can count on them to interpret what I'm getting at musically through a song, and that I rarely have to make any suggestions. This is rare, but it can happen with almost anyone, provided you've worked with them long enough and your communication is well developed. There can be resistance, and this is one of the unfortunate things that can be encountered when musicians get together—ego. It's surely something to deal with, and there are times when it seems that there is no end to the variety of difficult attitudes you can come across. It's really the same in all facets of life, only it always seems more magnified when it involves something as sensitive and volatile as music. I'm sure you'll have to go through your fair share of difficulties with other musicians, as well as your own emotions, over the course of your years as a player. Just remember it's all part of the game, and if the feeling can be put into your guitar playing, then you'll be better for it.

Getting Gigs

You may find yourself, if you are the band leader, also in the precarious position of having to find work for your band. This can be very time-consuming and stressful, but if your belief in yourself and your band is strong, it'll push you through the endless phone calls and auditions. When it comes to clubs, it often helps to have a demo tape of your band and any press you might have gotten along the way to impress the club owner. But sometimes it's the old story—you want to start working, but they always want to know where you've worked before!

And what if you haven't worked before? Well, there are many ways of getting your foot in the door. If you know the owner or the person who does the booking, that always helps. Even better, though, is knowing an already established band that will let you open a show for them. It's important not to scare them off by being *too* great, for one of the unfortunate truths in this business is that headliners, no matter at what level, always feel intimidated by good opening acts. Just wait till show time to "blow them away." This may not sit too well with the other band, but it will certainly stay in the minds of the club owner and the audience.

I can remember when I had my first "real" band at the age of sixteen. I was at college in Philadelphia, and we wanted to audition to play in a club in Woodstock, New York. We had heard that it was a great place to be noticed but that it was tough to break in. After all, we're talking about a small Catskill Mountain town with about twenty bands, and four clubs to support them! Anyway, we always had a real cockiness about such situations, and a true belief in ourselves and our music, so we decided to give it a shot. We showed up one cold fall evening at a club in Woodstock called the Sled Hill Cafe. It was not one of the fanciest places around, but it was frequented by some of the "heavies" in town. There was a very popular band playing there at the time, called Bang, with a great guitarist, Buzzy Feiten. They had no opening act, and we had no equipment with us, so I went up to Buzzy and asked him if we could sit in between sets using *their* equipment! I sure was bold, but he answered yes, and we proceeded to play a fine, if a little nervous, set. We felt hampered by the fact that we had to use someone else's equipment that night, and we played only about three songs, but the rounds of applause we received were well worth it.

I had left our phone number with the club owner, and waited for weeks for the phone to ring. It never did, but about a month later, we made another trip up to the club, and he went crazy as soon as we walked in the door! It seemed that he had lost the number but was in love with our music and wanted us to appear there regularly. Well, let me tell you, this felt as if we'd been signed to a major record deal, and we went right through the roof with joy! Needless to say, we became Philadelphia-to-Woodstock commuters, and played there quite often, developing a nice following. It didn't help my schoolwork any, but that wasn't nearly as important to me as getting my playing heard by the right people. The band went through some personnel changes that year, though we did keep playing in Woodstock. I eventually got noticed by people in town who really had some influence and were able to introduce me to musicians who made records and to a more "legitimate" musical life-style. The following year, at the very young age of eighteen, I left school and actually went up to Woodstock to live. As it turned out, this move was made a little prematurely, as I really knew no one there and had a hard time breaking into one of the musical "cliques" that permeated the scene there. As fate would have it, though, the following year—after I had moved back to New York City—brought me the most work in Woodstock, so much so that I was a regular on the bus!

Timing is everything in the music business, and it's crucial that you fight to be heard every step of the way. You'll never know who's out there listening and what they're looking for at the moment. This proved itself time and time again throughout my career, and it has always seemed that one good thing has led to another. Follow all leads, get phone numbers, have cards made up with either your name or the band's on it to give out, and generally be on the watch for what can help *you*. I really believe in always thinking *beyond* your current situation. This is not to say that there must always be a "greener grass" attitude on your part, but more that you should have higher horizons on your mind. Those gigs where I was playing my heart out with my band were also vehicles for me to have my guitar playing heard by other artists with whom I might enjoy working. I would also suggest "sitting in" with or jamming with as many other players as possible. This is important to your development as a musician, as well as a chance to be heard by others who might want to use you for a gig. I can remember one late-night jam in Woodstock that gave birth to my recording career with all the sessions I got as a result! So keep your ears open for where the hot spots are to play with other musicians, and make sure to be there as much as you can. If you're good enough, one good gig will keep leading to another.

Recording (Cutting Your First Demo)

The first time you set foot into a recording studio and begin to make music, the whole situation may really shock you. I know it shocked me, because making records in a studio is a much different discipline from live playing; in fact, they are like night and day. This studio-versus-live question is a tough one to deal with, but it's something most musicians eventually have to face and try to conquer. There are, of course, some types who thrive on the "under the microscope" way of recording and who abhor live gigs, but they are rare indeed, and their music usually suffers from sounding too "antiseptic." What you first want to capture in the studio and on tape is that same freshness that you have when playing live. In other words, it's like an actor trying to be *himself* in front of the camera.

As a band, you'll certainly want to go into the session as well rehearsed as you can be. This doesn't mean you should plan out every note—you should leave some room for creative ideas to happen in the studio—but the band, particularly the rhythm section of bass and drums, should be "tight." Remember, the studio is expensive, and you want to maximize your time and effort.

Because you are putting your music down on tape, you will be striving for a certain degree of consistency and perfection, so you might want to do several "takes" of a song so you can decide which one you want to keep. I always recommend keeping the first take of anything, if you can, because this is a special moment, when you are putting out all you've got, and your attitude is as positive and fresh as it can be. I'd say that seventy-five percent of all the solos and fills I've done on records and demos have been first-take jobs! Make sure the recording engineer has the tape rolling when you're playing something new, for he just might be recording the "keeper."

When recording a demo for your band, try to put your best material on it. This, of course, depends on the kind of band you are and what your goals are. If your main hope is to play weddings and Bar Mitzvahs, you may want to record some of your versions of other people's hits, show tunes, oldies, etc., to show what a versatile show you can put on. In fact, many bands these days are turning to video demos so the client can now see as well as hear you. If your band does its own material, you should obviously stress this in your demo, but you may also want to include an original treatment of a well-known song or a forgotten hit of days gone by. On my second album, the two songs that got the most airplay were my versions of "When a Man Loves a Woman" and "Poor Side of Town," both songs that I had grown up loving and had wanted to record for years. Keep this in mind, and try to find some interesting "cover" tunes that you may want to record and make fresh again. I have always found this to be a very rewarding means of expression, and, in fact, my albums have always been about forty percent cover tunes. Again, try to keep the songs on your demo down to a precious few—three, maybe four at the most. This will help to keep the attention of the listener, who may have to hear dozens of demos every day!

Financially speaking, it's important that you keep your demo in perspective. I know this can be hard, but there are times when you may be better off getting out of a bad situation, rather than continuing on and wasting time, energy, and money. I know I learned this lesson the hard way with my *first* demo session. It was in the summer of

1970, with my three-man power band, Steel. We were playing really well, we had unique songs, and we *thought* we had connections that could make us big stars. We recorded a demo in Asbury Park, New Jersey—where, by the way, a very young Bruce Springsteen used to hang out and watch me play. We walked into the place to find out that the main recording console, something I'd never even seen before, had broken down! What did this engineer do? He convinced us that we should all plug in, *direct*, to a small tape recorder. When I say *direct*, I mean without amplifiers at all. On stage we used almost seven huge amps, for a wall of sound that was *absolutely* essential to our music. Yet we looked at one another helplessly and went on with the ridiculous project. Even more ridiculous was that we intended to have this demo *pressed* into *records*! A demo is a very professional way of presenting one's music, but the stuff on ours was going to sound as if it was recorded in a tin can!

We all went down to a record-mastering place on Forty-second street and Broadway in New York City, not exactly the heart of the music world, and actually slept outside the studio while the record was being cut, our dreams fully intact. The engineer, who was going to end up getting all our hard-earned, hard-saved pay, even went so far as to come out in the hallway while we were sleeping and asked us if we really wanted to "go through with this." At this point we were hell-bent on seeing the project through! Needless to say, the demo got us nowhere. It was a hard-learned lesson, but not one we couldn't rebound from. Please don't let this kind of thing happen to you. Know what you're getting into before you commit your money.

As far as the act of recording is concerned, you should first lay down a good "rhythm track." This will give you a strong foundation over which to put vocals, lead guitar, or any other overdubs you might want to use. If the song requires a vocal, you or whoever will be doing the singing might lay down a "reference" vocal during the making of the rhythm track. This will give the musicians something substantial to "play off of" and will add to the spirit of the rhythm track. It will also serve as a good guideline when you do your lead-guitar overdubs if the "real" vocal hasn't been recorded yet.

As far as your own rhythm-track playing (rhythm guitar) is concerned, the old adage "less is more" could never be truer. There are the exceptions, of course, but on the whole, rhythm guitar parts should be sparse and augment the subtleties of the lead guitar. Just imagine yourself on a record date where you were playing lead guitar and the rhythm player was stepping all over your part. Needless to say, you wouldn't be too pleased, so you wouldn't want to find this same conflict within your *own* band. I know that as a young, up-and-coming player, I was so into my hot leads that I felt as if I'd been handcuffed when I had to play disciplined rhythm parts. The trick is to shift attitudes and to realize that all the juicy lead-guitar playing will soon follow. In the meantime, it's very important that you realize that the rhythm part must be disciplined, and for this you must learn to listen to the other musicians' parts. This will help in making you a better ensemble player, and you'll see what an art form rhythm playing really is!

When overdubbing your lead part, you, too, will have to "tame" your usually soloistic approach somewhat in the interest of creating a more consistent and well-communicated single-note track. It's a good idea to try to find lead guitar "hooks" that can be used throughout the song as musical statements. These hooks can sometimes be the highlight of the song, and many times the lead guitarist is called upon to create them on the spot. When this happens, you're really being enlisted as player, writer, and producer all at one time! Of course, there are many times when a song is already written around a hook line, and what you must play is more predetermined.

All of this can be a bit intimidating to the newcomer to such musical situations and may take some time to adjust to. Overdubbing can be a very lonely, misunderstood pursuit, and you really must put yourself mentally in front of an audience if you expect to put some real life into your playing. It helps sometimes to have other people in the studio whom you enjoy playing for and impressing, especially ones who are not easily impressed. This will cause you to reach back for that extra something that will make your guitar parts sparkle. When the final note has been played, though, *you* must be your own final judge. If you're happy with your part, that's really all that matters; if you're not, you'll probably never rest till it *is* right. I'm a firm believer in going for the best you can do, and I know that in the long run, you'll be a lot happier that you did!

Tips on Forming a Band and Making It Work

DO'S:

Try to find musicians who you like to work with, from ads, word of mouth, etc.

Rehearse as often as possible, but don't *over-rehearse*. Some things are better left to the live performing or recording situation.

Allow each member of the band an equal say in musical and financial matters.

Discuss openly any problems within the band together. No secrets.

Keep your equipment in good condition, to avoid breakdowns and technical problems that can occur at important times.

When making a demo or any recording, be sure to have all estimates and charges in *writing*, so you're not shocked with the bill!

When recording a demo, strive to capture the spontaneity in your music: don't over-produce.

DON'TS:

Don't forget that you are learning all the time.

Don't let egos get in the way of your musical relationships.

Don't let a bad gig get you down.

Don't be satisfied with a recording until all parts feel right to *you*.

Don't exaggerate your abilities to others. Let your playing speak for itself.

Don't expect success to come too easily. It *always* takes hard work.

Chapter Nine

A FEW FINAL THOUGHTS

This is the time that's hardest for me. We've only just begun a long and wonderful process for you, yet I have to say good-bye. It's now up to you to go on and make your own brand of music, breaking new ground as you go along. I know that when I was a young, developing player, I always made sure to set new goals for myself, no matter how small, and never to be satisfied with what I had known at the time. I can recall riding home on the bus from school when I was thirteen years old, with a new riff or lick in my head that I just couldn't wait to get home and attempt on the guitar. Obviously, I was a kid in love with music, and I felt so in touch with the guitar as an expressive tool that I was able to create and experiment even while away from the instrument physically. It's quite important that as a player who may be fantastic very early in his or her development, to avoid letting complacency set in. This can be very damaging in the long run. In fact, I can't think of *one* of all the neighborhood or school hotshots who really amounted to anything more on the guitar after high school, and these were the guys *I* was trying to impress! You should also remember, without paranoia, that there is always someone younger, better, and hungrier than you ready to take your place, and if you're involved in the highly competitive studio scene or in the record business, it's that much easier to hear their footsteps coming.

I can't emphasize enough the importance of going out in the "real world" and seeking out other musicians to play with. Playing alone has its place, but not until you have a chance to interact with others do you really see how you've progressed as a player. It's also important to make "practice" a word that you rarely use. I prefer to just think of it as pure fun and creativity, leaving the word *practice* for the students who sit with their guitars in neat rows in music schools that are in the business of assembly-line learning. Let it be a joy, for playing music is a lifelong learning process, as you, like most other musicians, will discover during the years to come.

Take note of your development, but avoid putting yourself "under the microscope." Let it all take place more naturally, allowing your own style to come about as a result. We can sometimes be guilty of overanalyzing what we're playing, to the point of ruining all of the innocence in what we're trying to express. Practice should be a discipline, but not a chore. We should set goals, but realistic ones. Especially if we want to keep a positive attitude. You also must be aware that growth comes in leaps and bounds, but it's also possible to suffer through some long dry spells in between. These times should not prompt you to abandon ship. All artists, no matter what creative field they're in, go through these periods in their lives. There are songwriters who won't write for a year, painters who may not pick up a brush, and writers who sometimes can't get past the first word. It happens to the best of us, and as a guitarist, you may find yourself not up to par for a while, then suddenly, you could hit a hot streak of positive development that will shake you! It's all part of the overall picture of you as a musician, and that's something to never lose sight of.

If you are a future star—and it's entirely possible that you are—I hope this book has helped to shed some light on some of the important elements in rock guitar for you, and that you're sufficiently inspired to go on to bigger and better things. We've gone over all the necessary basics, both physical and musical, that will get you off on the right foot, as well as headed off some potential bad habits. You should be well on your way to defining a personal sound for yourself, and if you keep at it, it shouldn't be too long before you're "out there" really doing it! All a guitarist can ever really hope for is to make himself or herself a happier, more fulfilled person through his or her instrument, and to make others feel, smile, and cry with him. All the rest of the stuff, well...that's the icing on the cake. Good luck!

DISCOGRAPHY

As a further aid in your development as a rock guitarist, I've here provided you with a list of what I feel is "essential listening." These are albums either by or containing the work of some of the most important guitarists who've ever lived, and represent a well-balanced "menu" for the aspiring player.

Rural Acoustic Blues

Robert Johnson: *King of the Delta Blues Singers Vols. 1 & 2* (Columbia)
Son House: *Father of Folk Blues* (Columbia)
Charlie Patton: *Founder of the Delta Blues* (Columbia)

Chicago Blues and Related Electric Blues

Elmore James: *Whose Muddy Shoes* (Chess)
Muddy Waters: All records (Chess)
Buddy Guy: *A Man and the Blues* (Vanguard)
Michael Bloomfield (*With The Paul Butterfield Blues Band*) (Elektra)
T Bone Walker: *Stormy Monday Blues* (Bluesway)
B. B. King: *Completely Well, Live and Well, Live at the Regal* (Bluesway)

Albert King/Otis Rush: *Door to Door* (Chess)
Magic Sam: *West Side Soul* (Delmark)

Country Rock

Carl Perkins: *Greatest Hits* (Columbia)
Merle Travis: *The Best of Merle Travis; The Merle Travis Guitar* (Capitol)
Clarence White: (with The Byrds) *Younger Than Yesterday; Easy Rider* (Columbia)

Rhythm and Blues

Chuck Berry: *Chuck Berry's Golden Decade* (Chess)
Bo Diddley: *Go Bo Diddley; Have Guitar Will Travel* (Checker)

Rock

Jeff Beck: *Truth; Beck-Ola; There and Back; Blow By Blow* (Epic)
Eric Clapton: *461 Ocean Blvd.* (RSO); *Slowhand* (RSO); *Bluesbreakers*, (London) *Fresh Cream; Disraeli Gears; Wheels of Fire*, (ATCO) With Derek and the Dominoes: *Layla* (ATCO)
John Lennon and George Harrison: all Beatles records and solo lp's.
Jimi Hendrix: *Are You Experienced?; Electric Ladyland; Axis; Bold as Love* (Reprise)
Jimmy Page: all Led Zeppelin albums
Keith Richards: all Rolling Stones records
Peter Townshend: all Who records plus *Empty Glass* and *White City* (ATCO)
John Fogerty: all Creedence Clearwater Revival records, plus *Centerfield*
Mark Knopfler: all Dire Straits records (Warner Bros.)
Eddie Van Halen: *Diver Down; 1984* (Warner Bros.)
Billy Gibbons: all ZZ Top records (Warner Bros.)
Duane Allman: all Allman Brothers records (Capricorn)

GLOSSARY

A capella: Singing without instrumental accompaniment.

Action: The height of the strings, which affects the ease with which the guitar can be played.

Barre: The use of one finger to cover two or more strings on the same fret.

Channel-switching: A feature of certain amplifiers that, at the touch of switch, enables you to go from one channel to another for different sounds.

Damping: The use of either hand to mute unwanted notes or sounds.

Dissonance: When notes are discordant, or tend to "clash" with one another.

Downstroke: When the stroke of the pick is down, *away* from you.

Fifth: The note of a key or a chord that is five notes away from the root note in the root note's major scale.

Flat: When a note is below a given pitch. The opposite of "sharp."

Fret: The metal bars crossing the guitar's fingerboard.

Fretting: Pressing down on the strings between the frets.

Hammer-on: Hitting the string from above the fretboard with a finger of the fretting hand. Usually created after a note is sounded. The opposite of a pull-off.

Harmonics: The bell-like tones that can be created at specific points along the string by lightly touching the string directly over the fret, then releasing the finger just after the string has been plucked.

Lick: Musician's lingo for a short musical phrase consisting of a few notes.

Major third: The note that exists tow whole-steps away from the root note that defines a chord as sounding "major." The third note of any major scale.

Minor third: the note that lies one and a half steps away from the root that defines a chord as being "minor." The third note in a minor scale.

Overdubbing: Recording on a separate track in a multitrack recording studio; playing one part to fit with other, already recorded instruments.

Passing notes: Those notes that lie between designated notes of a scale, used to "pass" from one position to another.

Picking: The act of sounding notes on the guitar with the plectrum, or pick.

Pickup: The device that lies beneath the strings of the guitar between the bridge and neck that translates the sounds of the strings into electronic impulses, which are transmitted to an outside source, such as an amp.

Piggyback amplifier: Any amplifier that consists of an amplifier and a separate speaker cabinet.

Power Chord: A partial chord form used primarily in rock and heavy metal that contains the root and the fifth of the chord but rarely includes a major or minor third.

Pull-off: The act of creating a new note by taking a finger *off* the string in a downward "plucking" manner. The technical opposite of a hammer-on.

Reverb: An effect built into many amps that creates an echolike sound by the use of a small chamber with internal springs.

Root: The note of a key or scale that defines the key one is in. Therefore A is referred to as the root note of the key of A, or of an A chord.

Sharp: When a note is above a given pitch. The opposite of "flat."

Slide Guitar: A form of guitar playing that originated in Hawaiian music and then was made popular by rural blacks in the deep South. The notes are created with either a metal tube, glass bottleneck, or similar object, which is laid across the strings to give the guitar's sound a haunting vocal quality.

String-bending: Raising the pitch of a string by pushing it *up*, toward you, or *down*, away from you.

Suspended Chord: A chord that contains a note such as a fourth or a second that is *not* part of the original chord's note grouping, which is then "overlayed" over the original chord.

Treble: A note or sound that is in the higher range of the musical spectrum. A bright, high-end sound.

Truss Rod: A rod, usually made of metal, that runs the length of the guitar neck to help maintain the neck's alignment. Usually adjustable.

Upstroke: Any picking motion that strikes the strings as the pick moves up, *toward* you. The opposite of a *downstroke*.

Vibrato: The wavering, sustaining sound that is created by a subtle change of pitch caused by movement of the fretting finger.

Vibrato Bar: An attachment to the bridge of some guitars that lowers the pitch of the strings when it is pressed down.

ABOUT THE AUTHOR

Arlen Roth has established himself as one of the most important and influential guitarists on today's music scene, working with such artists as Simon and Garfunkel, Bob Dylan, Phoebe Snow, Rick Wakeman, John Prine and Don McLean.

Through his many books and as the founder and producer of the internationally acclaimed HOT LICKS video and audio instructional tape series, Roth has introduced a whole new generation to the joys of rock guitar.

Roth has recorded four critically acclaimed solo albums and was awarded the 1979 Montreux Award for Best Instrumental Guitar Performance. He is a featured monthly columnist for *Guitar Player* magazine and most recently served as a special guitar consultant for the film "Crossroads."

ROCK IS HERE TO STAY...
SO STAY IN TOUCH WITH THE HOTTEST ROCK STARS!

A behind-the-scenes look that is sure to please even the most well-informed fan